The
Literacy of Belief:
An Autoethnography on Strategies
for Steering Your Mind

The
Literacy of Belief

*An Autoethnography on Strategies
for Steering Your Mind*

Uju C. Ukwuoma

REGENT PRESS
Berkeley, California

Copyright © 2020 by Dr. Uju C. Ukwuoma
[Paperback]
ISBN 13: 978-1-58790-486-8
ISBN 10: 1-58790-486-1
[Hardback]
ISBN 13: 978-1-58790-535-3
ISBN 10: 1-58790-535-3
[E-Book]
ISBN 13: 978-1-58790-488-2
ISBN 10: 1-58790-488-8
Library of Congress Control Number: 2019957018

Publisher's Cataloging-In-Publication Data

Names: Ukwuoma, Uju C., author.
Title: The literacy of belief : an autoethnography on strategies for
   steering your mind / Uju C. Ukwuoma.
Description: First Edition. | Berkeley, California : Regent Press, [2020]
Identifiers: ISBN 9781587904868 (paperback) | ISBN 1587904861
   (paperback) | ISBN 9781587904882 (ebook) | ISBN 1587904888
   (ebook)
Subjects: LCSH: Belief and doubt. | Self-actualization (Psychology) |
   Self-consciousness (Awareness) | Cultural awareness.
Classification: LCC BD215 .U39 2020 (print) | LCC BD215 (ebook) |
   DDC 121.6--dc23

While the stories in this book are true, some names and identifying
information may have been changed to protect the privacy of individuals,
groups, and other legal entities.

Cover Design: Mark Weiman
Images: Uju Ukwuoma

First Edition

1 2 3 4 5 6 7 8 9 10

Manufactured in the U.S.A.
REGENT PRESS
Berkeley, California
www.regentpress.net

Dedication

I have put almost my entire life into studying belief. The truth is that it has not been easy. Now, my goal is to break the process into smaller, more manageable pieces. I have seen that the circumstances we create and those that are not of our making contribute to the outcomes we experience. Some believe that humans should go with the motion and accept whatever life brings. Others think we should influence the movement to shape the aftermath of life. Many people do not care about life and what it brings. However, their lack of care does not preclude life from bringing what it brings. Some people do not worry about life because they believe that a higher power is in control. In spite of where they stand, many people of different beliefs are exercising their power to think. They are also using their innate ability to believe. Their thoughts and beliefs guide their behavior to determine the direction their lives take. Such people are literate in the art of living. Thus, I dedicate this book to all thinkers and believers who are knowingly and unknowingly modeling the *Literacy of Belief* every day.

Table of Contents

Prologue

"**M**y flight leaves in 45 minutes." "See you tomorrow, buddy." "Let's catch up over a meal in two days." "Can we discuss that over coffee later in the week?" "I will be there next month for the event." These are some of the things we say to one another without any actual reason to ensure they will happen. Be that as it may, we know it can be tough to accurately guarantee what will happen in the next minute. Why then do people make such commitments about future events? Do we have absolute control over how things will turn out? While it appears that we are not able to control things, I have found that people enter into such obligations with one another because of what they believe. Although we are not always aware, we believe we will be alive and in good health to fulfill our commitments. Our ape-like predecessors were different due to their fixed behavioral patterns. As such, only humans are capable of reasoning in such a manner.

In the absence of insanity, we can produce sensations, images, or ideas in our minds and, eventually, experience them precisely as we envisioned. In addition to the ability to visualize and conceptualize, human beings possess will-power, which enables them to actualize what they have imagined. For many years, I explored what would happen if we extended such capability to other areas of our lives. The exploration helped me to understand the importance of asking appropriate questions about life.

Ask yourself, for example, am I living the life of my visualization or imagination? Even if your answer is in the affirmative, it is essential to know that you can do better because life offers lots of room for improvement. Life has several initiatives in the offing for us. There are more good people in this world than we think. Many people from around the globe are sending positive thoughts and wishes of prosperity to other people in the world. Billions of people would jump at the opportunity to be of assistance to others. Life is much more than the bickering, hatred, and discrimination witnessed in some places. The political turmoil and religious bigotry we see around us are only isolated events. Life is a vast treasure awaiting discovery. Using a non-academic, easy to read narrative, this book documents over 25 years of my quest to understand how human thoughts and beliefs influence human outcomes. I posit that genetics and other factors influence what happens to us, but it is our imagination that breeds our beliefs, and we demonstrate what we believe through our behavior. My postulation implies that multiple forces contribute to what we experience as human beings. However, it is what we think that shapes our beliefs, and how we conduct ourselves is a reflection of those beliefs. As such, our thought pattern incubates what we desire and determines what we get in life. It follows that our current situation reflects what we or others have thought and believed in the past. As a result, the things we are thinking and believing are either taking us closer to or alienating us from a better outcome. I have concluded that we can think our way to a better life or circumstance by reevaluating our thoughts and our beliefs, including the decisions and actions we take.

In order to achieve such a feat, however, we have to become belief literate. Being belief literate means embracing a 3-step process I have developed and called *Belief Literacy Steps (BLS)*. First, identify where you are and the thoughts you have regarding the circumstances you want to change. Second, evaluate your opinions and beliefs about the circumstances and define where you want to be. Finally, design and implement appropriate steps to take you to your desired destination. Most of us are drastically unaware of our level of understanding of our belief system, but you will be able to list and explain the three-pronged *BLS* after reading this book. I also hope you will take those steps daily to steer your mind to your desired destination. Many people, especially effective teachers and engaged students, have taken *BLS* unconsciously and experienced great results. If taken consciously, *BLS* can and will lead to a significant payoff.

section one

CHAPTER 1

Belief is Essential in Life

We often become what we think, believe and do, but sometimes neither what we thought nor believed or did determines what we become.

*M*y uncle continued to treat my father as his son and baby brother many years after my father married my mom. To my beloved uncle Bryan, his three younger brothers required a lot of guidance from their eldest brother. It did not matter that each of the younger brothers was over the age of 45, married, and with teenage daughters and sons. Three of my uncles who were younger than uncle Bryan, had left our native land more than 20 years ago. Two of them have houses in big cities which they call home. Uncle Bryan's younger brothers visit the village only on weekends, festive periods, or during family reunions to check on their eldest brother. One of the four brothers has traveled to many countries in Europe and the Americas as a sailor and civil engineer. The other has received some western education but settled as a businessman in a significant commercial city. The third and youngest relocated to the United States for college education on an all-expense-paid scholarship by the then colonial, Posts and Telegraphs (P&T) department. Such credentials contrasted with the traditional way of life, in which my grandparents and great grandparents raised uncle Bryan and his three brothers in our rural and agrarian West African community in the early 1920s.

Growing up, I noticed that uncle Bryan played daddy to my father and his younger brothers. My father said that uncle Bryan assumed the role of a father as their parents aged, as expected in their culture. It was customary for older siblings and members of the community to take care of younger ones. I saw my parents care for my grandparents, and I also witnessed my grandparents caring for my great grandparents. There was not, and there is not such a thing as elderly people's homes like we have in the United States. People live together till old age, and they pass away still living with their kith and kin. As such, I was not just my father's son. I was also the son of my uncles and all of the elderly members of my extended family.

So, I cheerfully respected and ran errands for all elderly male or female members of our family. Respect was a crucial principle in the community. As kids, being respectful was expected of us; it was non-negotiable. Age seemed to earn people respect; the older you were, the more your chances were of being respected. However, everyone expected more respect from male family members than females. Such expectation was important because males were believed to be responsible for advancing the family legacy. Male family members worked more on family farms and businesses. Our sisters were respected, but the boys were groomed to become the breadwinners and authority figures of their future families.

Out of respect and my family's expectation of a higher standard of character, my male cousins and I followed instructions without hesitation. We respected all older adults, including aunts, elder brothers, elder sisters, grandparents, great grandparents, fathers, inlaws, mothers, and uncles in the village, no questions asked. Our elders deemed us as respectful if we did whatever they asked of us without hesitation or grumbling. Elders often asked us to bring firewood from forests. On some occasions, elders asked us to go to the village stream and fetch water for childless widows. The elders would also ask us to work in the family farmlands. Sometimes, they requested us to write letters for family members whose sons and daughters resided in cities that were far away from our community.

The most critical way of showing respect was by following the family's belief systems. Like other members of our community, my immediate and extended family members had many essential traditions that were centered on belief. Some followed the Christian faith. Others followed

Hinduism and Islam. Uncle Bryan was a hardcore ancestral worshiper, which I did not understand until after about 20 years of studying him. The remainder of uncle Bryan's brothers belonged to four organizations, which family members termed "Secret Societies." My older cousin, a Hindu, applauds himself as being among the first set of Krishna devotees in West Africa. His entire family follows the Hindu faith.

My mother taught me to stay away from family members who were Hindus, members of the Islamic faith, and those who belonged to secret societies. Mom took her adherence to the Christian faith a step further by identifying as born-again Christian. To respect my mom, I stayed away from family members who were Hindus and those who belonged to secret societies, but not Islam. Besides the motherly admonition, I was not too fond of the restrictive lifestyles led by those who identified as members of secret societies. Also, I did not like my older cousin's hairstyle. He shaved his head, leaving a little at the back, which made him stand out from everyone in the community. His dress style was also different from ours. So, as a child, I overlooked such family members.

I participated in the belief systems of family members who were of the Anglican Communion, Roman Catholic, and Jehovah's Witnesses. I also exchanged ideas with those who were Born-again Christians or Pentecostals, Cherubim and Seraphim members, Muslims, and those tagged secret society members, at a tender age, of course without my mother's knowledge.

I did not understand much about the ancestral worship of uncle Bryan even though he was the most open-minded of my uncles and a consistent practitioner of his faith. He coordinated an event often slated for early April. Although I now possess a doctorate and have been teaching for over 25 years, I am unable to name or explain the precise meaning of that April ceremony in the English language. Each time I asked, I was told that it was just a family tradition. However, I have a vivid recollection of what occurred during the ceremony. I witnessed the occasion four times when I was between the ages of seven and ten. After that, I left home for a boarding school in the city and lost the opportunity to witness more of the event.

Uncle Bryan believes in ancestral worship with everything in him. To him and his cohorts, belief is essential in life, and we become what we believe, think and what we do. While I want to concur, I have seen that sometimes in life, what we neither believed nor thought or did, determines what we become.

CHAPTER 2

Ancestral Worship of Uncle Bryan

What we see contributes to the shaping process of our future.

Uncle Bryan yells out like a town crier around three in the afternoon of his chosen day of worship: *"The time has come! Everybody should come out! Let us commune with our ancestors! Let us use our brain to solve our problems! Let us fellowship with those who own us and those we own!"*

Upon hearing his voice, we rush out to see him holding a chicken (or rooster, I am not sure) in his left hand and a kitchen knife in his right. The legs of the rooster are tied together. Uncle Bryan buries the head of the rooster backward in between the wings as if he wants to suffocate the fowl. You can hear the cock panting as we gather in front of uncle Bryan, but he does not care. He swings the chicken above everyone's head, saying things like:

"Everybody will be alive. May God protect us. No evil shall

befall any of us! If early death is coming, it will take this cock. Death will not seek for any member of our family. May those who will tell us one thing and do another thing never come our way! May the eyes of our enemies be blind towards our progress. May the spirits who own our land eat this rooster! May we continue to escape automobile accidents because that is not how we will die! Because life moves in cycles, may the cycles of our market days protect us. May we be in harmony with the periods that separate our market cycles. May our activities revolve around the rhythms of those cycles! May we have a bountiful harvest! May the forces that maintain the rhythms in all the big trees around us defend us!"

He then calls the names of people in the family tree who have died, asking them to protect us. Upon completion of his utterances, he kills the cock by slashing the throat. He sprinkles its blood on a particular spot at the center of our family premises. There are four buildings on the premises of our immediate family. The most conspicuous is my father's duplex surrounded by three of his brothers' bungalows built in a circular form. Our family reserved the spot where uncle Bryan poured the blood of the rooster, for that purpose. No one steps on the spot or gets close to it in the morning while sweeping, no matter how clean you want to sweep the compound. Some dirty looking white chalks and moth-infested carved wooden objects surround the spot like trash. A raggedy looking piece of zinc covers the place so well that a visitor can overlook it for a garbage dump. In short, the spot appears like a disposal site.

Someone is delegated to cook the cock, probably uncle Bryan's wife or one of my cousins' mom. It always turns out to be very spicy but delicious chicken soup. That is my favorite part of the event because everyone eats the food, no matter how little you get.

While eating, uncle Bryan describes how everything around us has a rhythm and moves in cycles. He teaches us this point by encouraging us to place one of our hands on our chest to feel our heartbeat. My grandfather often added that we could become whatever we chose to be in life if we allowed our brain to direct us and if we learned to think and wait on the divine direction of our ancestors.

What thrilled me the most was the way uncle Bryan began his day. He usually sat in front of his house early in the morning, surrounded by many items: a little earthen pot containing kola nuts, alligator pepper, white chalk, and other things I did not recognize. He also had a type of gin that had more than 95% alcohol and an object that looked like an elephant tusk, which, according to him, represented some idols. I enjoyed listening to his chants. He held a piece of chalk in one hand and his high proof dry gin on the other. He threw parts of the chalk to the ground, splashed some of the gin, made some poetic recitations as if he was addressing someone physically present there, and gazed at the imagined being.

"God, the creator. God, who created everything and knows all he created, whereas his creation does not know him, come and have

some chalk. *Come and rub off of this chalk — God of my previous seven lives. God of my present life, this is chalk. Come and rub. A new day is here, and mornings are powerful. As we open our doors, we open our hearts and mouths. Please, come. It is the reciprocity of respect that leads a woman to give birth to her kind. I have come to you this morning because another day is here. What I have in my hand is chalk. I also have an alcoholic drink. All of you should, please, take some chalk and have some drinks. Whoever I have called, should please call his kind. No one should come alone."*

As he poured drinks on the ground, he reaffirmed: *"Land is the same, that is why people step on it all over the world. I beckon you to come and take your share. My ancestors, I call on you this beautiful morning to come and drink. My late great grandparents come and rub some chalk."* At that point, he pronounced the names of more than twenty of his ancestors and asked them to join him.

"What I am asking is for everything to be well with us. Men and women should encounter lots of goodies. We do not want to kill anyone, but anyone who wants to kill us will die. The host of water spirits, I did not forget you, please come and have some chalk, come and have some drinks. All the spirits living in the waters, near and far, come and eat with us. None of you is exempted. I insist that anyone I have called should call his mates so we can be complete, because there is strength in unity. Please, all of you, put your hands together to prevent war in our land. Chalk is holy. Chalk is white in color. We use chalk to get good things. Chalk has no association with impurities. All of

you should remove impurities in the lives of all members of our family. May our stars shine. May the eagles in us arise."

As he rubbed the chalk on his head, eyes, ears, mouth, chest, hands, and legs, he continued to affirm.

"Our brain will function properly by thinking good and peaceful thoughts, our eyes will not see evil, our mouths will say good words, and our hearts will not harbor evil thoughts because it is also the heart of God."

With his hands lifted to the sky, he continued, *"Our hands will work so we can have enough food, our legs will not take us to bad places."*

Finally, he listed all the four market days that constitute one week in the Igbo tradition and declared that those days would bring good tidings.

"It shall be well for us on Eke day, on Orie day, on Afo day, and on Nkwo day in the name of God Almighty, the creator of Heaven and Earth."

Lifting a kola nut to his mouth, he chants, fluently, in the Igbo language as he did with the chalk: *"The creator of Heaven and Earth, the One who lives above us but has given us the Earth, here is kola nut. I present this kola nut as thanks for the life you have given us. I thank you for good health; for granting to us the gifts of knowledge, wisdom, and understanding. Accept my thanks for the boundless opportunities you have given our sons and daughters. I thank you for my family, for my friends, and for my well-wishers. Oh, merciful one! I also thank you because of my enemies. I thank you because of those who say*

12

we cannot drink water and keep the cup. I thank you because the ground will sweep them away in due time. Please, come and eat kola nut. Eat and show me that you have answered my prayers. You know what my heart desires, so please make my desires come to pass. To you, my Chi (personal God), I present this kola. I request you accept this kola nut. Please, accept this kola nut on behalf of the gods and the angels."

Making friendly gestures as if he is in the company of another, uncle Bryan utters: *"Please, present my request to them. I am a mere mortal; I am weak, but you are my strength. I am requesting for your spiritual and physical guidance. Cover us with your kindness and protection. Keep our enemies from tormenting us and shatter every impediment that hinders our way. I declare that we are free from all troubles. We are free from all dangers. May your blessings come quickly. Let the doors of opportunity open for our children. May the sun shine your glory into our lives, and may it blanket our spirits like a dew. Ancestors, I present this kola nut to you. I ask all of you to receive my offering of kola nut, for I am your child. I am your blood. Exit the realm of spirits and eat kola nut. I know that you dwell in the spiritual realm where favor and prosperity are in abundance. Bring to us blessings of happiness, the longevity of life, and success during your trip. May we have them in abundance in this generation till our seventh arrives. The gods and goddesses of our land, please come and enjoy this kola nut."*

He recites the names of many shrines and deities and invokes them, *"Take this kola nut to the spirits whose names*

I am yet to call. All you spirits whom I am unable to see, please eat kola nut. To those of you who are at my front (he extends his hand forward), eat kola nut. To those spirits who protect me at my back (he stretches his hand behind him), take kola nut. To you spirits at my left and right-hand sides (he turns his hand both ways before continuing), I know you protect me from invisible forces and danger, so, take kola nut."

Finally, he breaks the kola nut and swings the pieces around his head, saying, *"I hope that you have answered my prayers. Please, show me some signs. I am like a child who bathes only on his tummy. I know nothing. I trust your divine direction. Please, manifest your powers."* He then eats a piece of the kola nut and throws the rest away for the spirits.

He performs a similar ritual, but with the seeds of alligator pepper, which he refers to as a cleansing agent. While holding a couple of the seeds and slightly exposing them, he places them all over his body, saying, *"By the touching of this alligator pepper all over my body, may all negativity leave my body."* Moving meticulously from his forehead, he makes his way down to his face and chest until he reaches his legs. Finally, he raises the hand with the alligator pepper and moves it anticlockwise four times above his head and, after that, throws them away. He engages in these rituals every day. Having observed uncle Bryan for 20 years practicing his beliefs, and considering what I learned in the process, I now know that what we see contributes to the shaping process of our future.

CHAPTER 3

Our Behavior Reflects Our Beliefs

What humans believe shows up in human actions, even when humanity does not understand their beliefs.

One of our most valued family traditions in Africa is the acquisition of Western education. As young children, we showed respect for family traditions and values by attending school. I enjoyed going to school. All that was required of me in school was to attend classes and learn. Schooling was easy because my parents provided for me abundantly. I did not have to worry about clothes, foods, or school fees and tuition. However, the multiplicity of belief systems at home influenced everything I encountered at school. An elementary school was a couple of miles away from our family premises, and we were mandated to attend school. If any child was at home by seven forty-five in the morning of a school day, he or she would hide from adults within sight. There was no credible reason to be at home during school hours, so children had to hide from the prying eyes of elders. In short, no one should notice you at home when you are expected to be at school. At times, some of us were sent home early as punishment for fighting at school. I was always the one everyone expected to see at home because of troubles at school, but I never returned home.

I had a habit of hiding in one of the bushes behind the school to wait for school to be over in the afternoon. I always joined other students on their way home as if nothing had happened. No one ever saw me at home during school hours or even knew about my punishment for fighting at school. Fighting was a sign of disrespect and it brought insult to our family. Unfortunately, no matter how I concealed what happened at school, the news always reached my aunts, father, mother, or uncles. As a result, my father spanked me regularly for fighting at school. Spanking was a reasonable kind of corporal punishment at home and in school, which I received on an almost daily basis during my formative years. The unbelievable part was that my dad never allowed me to explain how or why the altercation ensued at school. While spanking me, my dad always said that I disrespected our family at school or that I threw the family name to the mud by fighting.

Usually, the spanking began before he finished the sentence. In spite of the spanking, I considered him a good father who, more often than not, listened to me with a compassionate heart. All the same, his heart (or mind) did not have any room to hear explanations about why fighting was a compelling option at school. In spite of that, elementary school was fun for me. We sang songs and played a lot. We also cut grass in the school field, which we called manual labor. Sometimes, we worked at the school farm. Our teachers were helpful and told us folktales. We also learned how to speak, write, and develop communication skills in the English and Igbo languages. Igbo was the language of social interaction, while English was the language of classroom instruction. Because almost all of us struggled to speak English, those who included English into their regular speech were respected in class.

Our teacher once asked us to explain the meaning of breakfast in class. I remember how everyone laughed at me when I described it as food eaten by English people. A smarter boy in my class described it as the food consumed in the morning. He received a standing ovation. However, we never called our morning food by that name. Perhaps, the main point of the answer should have been *food*, which I pointed out in my description. Some people see breakfast as the food people eat at a particular time of the day, which British people call breakfast in their language. Others view breakfast as whatever you eat first after sleeping, akin to breaking your fast. Somehow, my teacher should have given me credit for describing breakfast as food. Silly me! I sound defensive. I goofed, yet many years later, I am rationalizing my answer. However, if such an incident occurred in my classroom today, I would give some credit to the student who mentioned food first in his or her description. No student would have laughed at or ridiculed any student in my class.

I trace my desire and love for teaching to my elementary school experience and the question about breakfast. Although my teacher and fellow students jeered at me in class, I was not worried. I believed that there were others in the class who did not mock or laugh at me. Those people were not my classmates. They were the people whose names uncle Bryan recited before he killed the rooster. I believed they were in the class with me, smiling and saying, *"You are doing a great job."* I considered them my fans and cheerleaders. That was the same impression I got from listening to discussions during that April family ceremony discussed in a previous chapter. I sincerely believed that I was not alone, even when I was by myself. I felt that those people who uncle Bryan called upon were always with me, although I did not see them physically. Such a notion taught me that our personal beliefs determine the outcomes we encounter. The things I witnessed and heard from uncle Bryan influenced the thoughts I had in the classroom under entirely different circumstances.

Unfortunately, I did not feel the presence of my fans and cheerleaders while in church on Sunday mornings.

Each time I walked into Sunday school, I felt an empti-
ness, which reminded me that my cheerleaders were ab-
sent. Their presence reemerged when I stepped out of the
church. It was fun, but I was not able to explain such feel-
ings or why I sensed the presence of some people named
during the April family event. At the successful completion
of elementary school, I headed to secondary school. The
formal education structure was called the 6-3-3-4 system.
You put in six years in elementary school, three years in
junior secondary, another three in the senior secondary
school, including a minimum of four years for a college degree. Similar to elementary school, secondary school was
fun. I enjoyed the academic challenges and enjoyed English
literature, a subject that introduced me to the importance
of printed words. Secondary school also brought the opportunity for smoking cigarettes and fighting when situations
called for settling scores using violence.

The most exciting part of that stage of my schooling
process was that family members did not hear much about
the fights that took place at school. I lived at a boarding
school in a faraway city about one hundred miles away.
The fun part about fighting was that you waited for whoever you planned to fight on his way home. Upon seeing
him, you would yell a question. *Am I the one you are in-
sulting?* At the same time, you would point your finger at
him and invade his personal space by getting very close.
The culprit would either apologize or scream back at you.

Apologies often came in a quiet and gentle tone, but they bolstered my ego and made me yell more before walking away. If he yelled questions at me, we had no other option but to fight. *What will you do if I insult you? Or What. Will. You. Do?* Upon hearing such a question, I knew that the person was as delirious as I was or even more insane. Such responses also indicated that he was ready to fight. So, I would shove him immediately, and we would start throwing punches. The principle objective was to be the first to get the other person to the ground. Once somebody is on the ground, a winner and a loser have emerged, marking the end of the brawl.

Most times, they beat the crap out of me, but I enjoyed the experience. There were times I apologized when I noticed that the person I wanted to fight had more troubles brewing in his head than I did. In spite of my foolishness at enjoying my combative display of violence through fighting, I continued to be a respectful child. I attended church every Sunday. It had to be any church, not my family church, because I was far from home. My fans and cheerleaders continued to disappoint me by not revealing themselves physically to help me fight. These unseen fans and cheerleaders relentlessly deserted me each time I walked into a church, as I stated at the start of this chapter. Ironically, I felt confident that I was not alone.

On a Tuesday afternoon at the school hostel, my hand began to shake profusely. It was probably my right hand,

and it continued to swing until my fellow students noticed. Mortified, I covered my hand with my blanket. Silently, I repeated the same poetic recitals of uncle Bryan and, instantaneously, my hand calmed.

With that immediate relief, I realized that my family's April event was not just about killing a rooster or sounding too philosophical for seven-year-old me. It was a powerful ceremony that offered protection to members of our family in line with uncle Bryan's assertions. A few weeks later, my hand began to shake again while I was with a group of classmates. With confidence, I recited uncle Bryan's poetic recitations, but my hand continued to shake. So, I bid my hostel mates goodnight and walked into my room. The next day my hand functioned like nothing had happened the previous night. During the holidays, I traveled with Henry, one of my classmates, to his village. On our first night, my hand began to shake again. I looked worried. So, Henry's father consoled me. He told me not to worry about my hand. To him, it was not a problem or any form of sickness.

With confidence, he explained that my hand shook because of my *Ikenga* (hereafter, a deity, family deity, or idol).

"What is that?" I asked in a distraught voice.

"It is about your power and strength," he responded. According to him, the deity was a good thing and not something to cause me unhappiness. The idol was the mediator between my personal God (known as Chi in Igbo

mythology) and I. Such perspective emanates from many Afro-traditional religions. Subscribers of such belief systems view various objects and statues as intermediaries between human beings and gods. Some adherents of such faith, like my uncle, exalt carved images because they consider those images as offering a quicker route to the gods. *Belief Literacy Steps* counters such reasoning. Our senses are capable of sending information to our brain to enable us to understand the world around us as well as figure out how to deal with complex issues. Be that as it may, some people have formed a habit of attributing things to the unknown which seems to give them leeway for avoiding responsibilities.

He informed me that I had to reach my God by means of an idol. "Sir, how can I have a different God from others? Why am I the only one with a shaky hand?" I queried, confused.

Instead of answering, he asked me another question: "Do you fight?"

"No, sir," I lied.

"Good! Do not fight, so you don't kill anybody. Also, make sure you do not punch anyone with that hand because anyone you hit will die, and you will go to prison," he warned.

The thought of killing someone with my bare hands and going to jail frightened me. There and then, I decided to stop fighting. I also decided to tell my family about my shaky hand. As such, I left my friend's place for my village the next day. I believed that Henry's father was not capable of answering all of my questions. Once I returned home, I explained the ordeal to uncle Bryan.

"Have you told your father?" he questioned.

"No, sir," I replied timidly. He expressed surprise that I delayed in informing him, my father, or any of my uncles.

After scolding me for about half an hour, he confirmed that my hand shook because of the deity. Also, he told me it was time to appease my idol. I did not fully comprehend his point of view, but his explanations helped to shape my understanding of family idols.

CHAPTER 4

The Dynamics of Belief

What we say and do in the absence of insanity
when we are not acting or pretending, depicts
our belief systems.

"Why me, uncle?" I asked. He ignored my question and sent for uncles Julius and Ephraim. My uncles gave conflicting accounts of my relationship to the deity. I sensed confusion. However, all of my uncles agreed that a spiritual intervention was required to mollify Ikenga, the source of my strength. I deduced from their conversation that the idol was the channel for reaching what was responsible for my predicament, for lack of a better word. My friend's father was right. So, they sent for a native doctor. Many believe that native doctors have powers to control spirits. No one bothered to inform my father. He would learn about the development when he returned from his expedition to the city to teach college students.

My uncles are my fathers, and they have my best interest at heart, I mused. To them, it took more than a biological father to raise a child. Upon arrival, the native doctor threw some cowries to the ground several times. He picked the cowries, shook them in his hand, and threw them back on the floor. It appeared he had nothing else to do than pretend he was rolling dice. His routine consisted of picking the cowries, shaking them in his hand with a closed palm, and throwing them to the ground. When the cowries were on the floor, he looked at them as if he expected them to talk. He uttered something similar to uncle Bryan's poetic recitals. He sounded different, though. Because I was taking the Igbo language and Igbo literature as subjects at school, it was easy to understand his proverbs. He said things like: "Sudden occurrences defeat a brave man, but you also know a brave man when unforeseen circumstances happen."

He also pointed out, like uncle Bryan, that the ground was the same all over the world because it had sand, and everybody marched on the sand. Finally, he suggested to my uncles what they should buy, as if he were a medical practitioner prescribing medication. Two goats, two roosters, kola nuts, alcoholic drinks, some leaves, the outermost layers of shrubs, and parts of some trees. The shrubs and tree parts were from trees our people considered sacred. The list also included a four-faced wooden image of the idol. The native doctor insisted that my spiritual work required a four-faced image of the deity because I was a powerful native doctor. Having said that twice, I

looked at him, puzzled at the notion of being a native doctor without my knowledge. He looked at me like a crook
and quietly uttered, "In your previous life, my son." As
such, more items were needed to appease the gods on my
behalf. Appearing serious and with a disconcerting smirk,
he told my uncles some of the things I did in my past life
with the shaky hand.

"If he craved coconuts, all he had to do was point
his trembling hand in the direction of the exact coconut
he desired. Whichever coconut he pointed at fell to the
ground." He sounded stranger than fiction to me. For
once, something in me wanted to punch his face, but the
idea of killing someone and going to prison prevented me.

Nevertheless, my uncles gave him some money, and he
left. He returned after about two hours with the items on
his list. In my presence, the native doctor killed the goats
and roosters. He sprinkled their blood on the ground.
Also, he made a little hole in the ground and put two small
tree branches inside. Afterward, he recited narrative-like
incantations inviting various gods to commence the process of eating food.

"*Amadioha*, the famed Igbo god of thunder, it is time
for you to consume a goat. Come and eat fowl, come, and
drink alcoholic drinks. *Ala*, the ground upon which we
stand, have some drinks," he chanted. He poured more
alcoholic beverages on the ground. After a series of chants
and cleaning the blood of the goat and cocks on my left

hand, he asked the deity to be my guide. He hit my chest with one cock and slammed an entire goat on my body in an offensive manner. Again, I felt like punching and pushing him to the ground. Finally, he added the statue of the deity to the dirty spot in the middle of our family premises. He instructed my uncles to grant the idol food, drinks, and the blood of animals periodically.

Furthermore, he directed them to kill goats, roosters, or cows for the deity during critical events in my life. I went back to school a day after the ritual and continued with my usual activities. Surprisingly, I felt more energetic and confident without any urge to fight. My hand did not shake again till the end of my final year of junior secondary school and for the entire three years of senior secondary.

Being belief literate has taught me that idolatry and the belief systems of uncle Bryan worked for me, not because of their effectiveness, but because of my belief. I believed they would work and they worked. However, in the first year of my senior years, I failed our third term examination. The third term examination determined who would repeat a class or advance to a new level. It was the yearly promotion exam. Our school had a ridiculous policy of announcing the three best and three worst students academically on the final day of school in the school hall. So, it was on that day I heard my name among the worst three students of the year. The worst three are also known as those who carry the school on their heads. The news came to me as a shock, but Paul, another of my class-mates, worsened everything. He walked up to me as we left the hall and asked, *"Do you know that killing a king is better than embarrassing him?"* I did not answer his question, so he laughed and asked me if the class was weighty on my head. At that moment, I wished that the ground would open and swallow me so the students would have something else to discuss.

For the first time in my life, I was afraid to return home for the holidays. So, I decided to die. On my way home, I stopped at a pharmacy and bought 30 tablets of a sleeping pill. We called such stores chemist shops. A doctor's prescription was not required to purchase medications. Any medicine you could pay for was yours for the asking. Forty-five minutes before I got home, I took 10 of those pills. Before I reached our family compound, I began to stagger. I made it to our parlor and into the welcoming arms of my mom before drifting into a heavy slumber. Two days later I awoke, only to see our house crowded with people who wanted to know my whereabouts and what I had consumed. I could not comprehend why nearly every member of our community was congregated in my name. Some suggested that my parents rush me to a hospital. Others questioned the rationale: *"He is awake. Why does he need a doctor? He probably overslept."*

My mother reiterated, *"They've killed my son!"*

She began to spoon-feed me. My father instructed her

to bring me to the presence of everyone so I could explain what had happened to me. From my room upstairs, I could hear them deliberating in the downstairs living room on what they would do concerning me. Some said it might be some evil spirits that made me sleep for so long. Our house became even more congested as more people traipsed in. Amidst the confusion, my mother snuck me out of the house.

"We are going to Nkwerre to see Daddy," she said to me. "Daddy" was the name we fondly called the founding Reverend of my mom's church, one of the largest in Africa. I narrated to Daddy how I wanted to end my life because I had failed my third term exam. Everyone in the room was shocked that I could do such a thing. So, Daddy asked for a cane and told me that I needed some whipping. As I wrote in a previous chapter, spanking was a reasonable kind of corporal punishment at home and in school, which I received on an almost daily basis in my younger years. So, I quickly stretched my right hand in obedience. Holding the little stick firmly, Daddy raised his right hand, ready to lash me.

As seconds progressed to minutes, I awaited the first stroke. The silence was deafening; I could hear a pin drop. Daddy held his hand in the air for about five minutes. I saw the surprise on everyone's face. When he lowered his hand, he gave the cane to one of his assistants to throw away. Then he told the appalled bystanders that God instructed him not to flog me. I brought down my hand, but

I did not understand what he meant.

"You will do so well in school that you will forget that you once failed an exam," he said to me. *"You will also reach the peak of the academic ladder. Perhaps, that is why the devil wants to take your life."* He then told my mom to continue praying for me at our home. Finally, he prayed for everyone present and asked one of his assistants to give me some biscuits and soft drinks. My mom and I left the church for our home, but I remained perplexed.

In spite of all that happened, I was not fully aware of all of my family's belief systems. Also, I did not understand in its entirety what the family deity implied. Additionally, I did not comprehend the April ceremony or why uncle Bryan killed those innocent animals. I did not understand why Daddy said I would do well in school while I drowned in shame for not doing well on my exam. I did not know why my Hindu cousin had a unique hairstyle or moved in groups with other Krishna devotees. Notwithstanding, I continued to feel the impact of those belief systems in my life, negatively and positively. In other words, what I believed influenced what happened to me even when I understood little to nothing about such belief systems. Indeed, looking at the dynamics of belief now shows that what we say and do in the absence of insanity when we are not acting or pretending, depicts our belief systems.

CHAPTER 5

The Irony of Belief: Victimhood Spurring Creativity

May what I don't know ignore me as what I know recognize me.

*T*here were various agricultural roads in our village. My male cousins and I followed these tracks to farms and streams, from which we fetched water. I enjoyed taking strolls on these paths because it was a chance to see sacrificial items littered on the roadside. We often saw pieces of gum, candies, coins, and, on rare occasions, ornaments. I collected these items and used them to decorate my room. Before I obtained the trinkets, I would always repeat this: *"May what I don't know ignore me, as what I know recognize me."* My cousins would reprimand me, warning that I would run mad by touching sacrificial items. I chose to ignore their warnings.

I believed those items to be impotent and incapable of inflicting any real harm on me. In hindsight, I should've taken their admonitions to heart. Indeed, I engaged in such silly behavior because I was unaware that I was a victim of my beliefs. Many people, just like I was, can unconsciously become victims of their ideas. This consequence makes it imperative that we learn to be literate in belief. You are literate in belief when you have a clear understanding of the spiritual influence you have experienced throughout your life. Whether we acknowledge it or not, there are beliefs upon which our lives revolve. We do everything in our power to perpetuate these beliefs after forming them, because they influence our capabilities. Indeed, humans behave in this manner because of the pervasive and persuasive role of belief in our lives.

While my immediate and extended family consisted of individuals with various belief systems, they were very loving and united. They found a common ground in having guiding belief systems. As such, growing up in their midst helped to spur a quest for meaning in me. At a tender age, family members exposed me to the knowledge they believed would help me to find my meaning and understand the purpose of life. In spite of the variations in belief, I noticed that they shared a common view amongst themselves. Indeed, they believed in God — each family member had a different definition—evolution, creationism, reincarnation, the divinity of the supernatural, fate, the power of the human brain, and great reverence for the dead. Some professed the belief that the spirit of family members who have passed away continued to influence the affairs of those who remained.

Such a multiplicity of belief systems soothed anxieties and the troubles of life by changing the way I perceived things. As I reflect on those belief systems, I am tempted to conclude that they were nonsense, but I hesitate to do so because I learned so much from them. For example, I learned how to love my neighbor and understood that whatever I do to him or her directly, I do to myself indirectly. I learned how to meditate, which regulated my emotions. I developed a *possibility* mindset from observing a series of rituals and understanding the enormous power of the human brain. Also, I recognized early in life that there is a purpose for our existence on Earth.

Most importantly, being a part of many belief systems taught me how to understand and tolerate opposing views. Thanks to those belief systems, I now know that no one can control everything in life. However, *Belief Literacy Steps*, outlined in-depth in a later chapter, have taught me that human beings can lead successful lives by adhering to uncomplicated beliefs and using their brains correctly. An example of such uncomplicated knowledge is a belief in oneself, which mirrors a faith in your Source, God or Creator. Also, you can organize your life successfully by using your brain (or mind) appropriately through careful thinking. Because the human brain has been featured many times in this book, it is vital to say that I have been taught in school that the human brain is divided into two hemispheres, left and right. Our primate brothers and sisters, the chimpanzees (chimps), have a similar brain distinction. Scientists have also classified our brain into frontal, temporal, parietal, and occipital lobes, features that are similar to primates like the chimps.

In short, the majority of other mammals have the same brain makeup as humans, including the neocortex. While it is difficult to detect the basis of human distinctiveness in our brain, everyone agrees that we have the ability to self-reflect, unlike other mammals.

From a quick and furtive look at *Belief Literacy Steps (BLS)*, which is yet to come, we see that the core of *BLS* is two-fold. The first is that the greatest asset of every human being is the ability to self-reflect and rationalize, which mirrors the image and likeness of our creator. Secondly, the factors we reflect on or rationalize, often emanate from our beliefs. Thus, human beings ought to work on what they believe and how to regulate their thinking process to make headway in life. Such regulation would enable them to engage in thoughts that facilitate beliefs that build rather than those which destroy.

Another essential factor is the need to understand how the cortex of our brain interacts with what we believe. Without trying to sound academic or prescriptive, we need to realize that what we *think* is critical to how we live our lives. As a result, it is crucial to understand our beliefs. Similarly, we should watch what goes into our brain as a way to control our thinking process.

Accordingly, the strategy for understanding our beliefs and monitoring what goes into our minds is in a simple truth — ask the right questions. Ask yourself questions like, *What do I know about such and such issue? What are my beliefs regarding so and so? What do I see? How do I interpret what I see? What do I hear? How do I understand what I am hearing? What paradigm do I use to explain what I am smelling, tasting, or touching?* Now that you have recognized the importance of asking the right questions, would you rather have what you know to recognize you? If you answered in the affirmative it is also helpful to understand that what you know will protect you from the harm that may arise from what you do not know.

CHAPTER 6
Understanding Self-Belief

Asserting a belief in oneself is like following the precepts of your source unknowingly.

*A*fter completing secondary school, I went off to university. The power of Ikenga to calm the nerves in my hand made the deity a phenomenon I held in high esteem. Also, I believed that somehow, the idol was useful and could make someone abhor fighting and live a responsible lifestyle. However, everything changed in college. The urge to fight returned, and I made friends with guys who were much more troublesome than I. I began to smoke marijuana. We got a good supply from a place called *Kwali* – they grew excellent hemp naturally. I did not know how good the stuff we puffed was until I went to Europe as a student and later the United States. The stuff I smoked in many countries in Europe and North America were different. The weed in the Western world was different. They seemed to involve chemicals in the cultivation process. When you smoke such chemical infused weed on a Thursday, it fast forwards your brain, so you start living on a Sunday.

One day a fight broke out at a smoking joint near campus. We dispersed, hoping that it was over, but some folks reignited the conflict on our college campus. We were rounded up by school security, and three weeks later, school authorities expelled all 12 of us. I was not surprised when the disciplinary committee recommended expulsion. With the carefree lifestyle we lived on campus, I knew that anything could happen at any time. So, I made it a point of duty to write a university entrance examination every year in case I had to start over at another school. Starting over is an essential feature of *Belief Literacy Steps* because a cyclical process is involved. Indeed, it means to do it all over again. However, it often requires you to take a different approach. If you do not receive the outcome you expect, your next step should be to complete the steps all over again. As such, it was only a few weeks later before I entered another college. During my registration, I met Mike, also known as Micro Mike. We called him Micro because he was vertically challenged, or short.

However, height was the only area where he was lacking. Micro had an overabundance of guts and curiosity. He was strong-willed and could do anything he chose to in life. In short, Mike had the intellect of a wizard. He planned and executed hits with scientific precision. For my friends and I, the concept of *hit* was a neat way of saying fighting or attacking someone. Micro would later teach me about willpower and the power of a human mind. Mike emphasized the need for me to believe in myself. Punching my chest one evening, he told me that I was afraid of the unknown.

"You have to become a thinking man! Think, my brother!" he yelled. *"You are living your life shrouded in superstition! Your ideas about idols and your family's traditional ceremony are contaminating your mind! I suggest you believe in yourself because you have the power to do whatever you want to do in life!"*

"What a strange saying, how did I get such an ability?" I asked rhetorically. I didn't quite understand him, so I shared those ideas with Promise, another friend of ours. Mr. Promise was like me. He told me about a powerful deity with a shrine close to our campus. He insisted that such gods and goddesses were traditional judicial systems of olden days, also useful in modern times. What was his point? He believed I should have ignored Mike and his philosophy because such ideas were from smoking weed.

Nevertheless, Mike's proposition that I ought to believe in myself fascinated me. I felt as if I could control a belief in myself. So, I ignored the fact that Mike smoked more weed than all of us and had more meetings with him. I wanted to identify with his philosophical base. He introduced me to what we called spiritual exercise. Before we started the practice, we took a bath. Mike insisted that taking a shower facilitated physical cleansing and epitomized spiritual expurgation. It was not like our daily bathing, but there was nothing out of the ordinary in the process. We showered in the usual way, but shortly after starting, we uttered some words. For example, we said words like: *"I am cleaning my body now." "I am cleansing my mind." "I am washing from my head to my feet and every part of my body." "I will be clean." "I am becoming clean now." "I do not have any impurity because I am clean."* We also said things like *"All the negative thoughts in my mind are going away." "My mind is free from all troubles and worries."* After bathing, we usually dried our bodies with clean towels and perched nude at a quiet location. Mike and I often did this exercise in my room because I was alone in a large room with eight beds for eight students.

Other students did not want to live with me. Our warden scolded me and called me antisocial. However, my friends and I disagreed with the warden. The boy he did not see as social or sociable represented a blessing in disguise for 15 other students who did not have accommodation on campus. We allocated the beds to ourselves, two persons per bed. First-year students and seniors were top priorities when our warden assigned rooms on campus. As such, I allocated the bed spaces to my friends who did not get accommodation on campus because they were neither freshmen nor seniors. So, my room ended up housing 16 students who shared one thing in common. All of us were friends who were also members of the same fraternity. Micro was a fraternity official, but other frat members were not part of our spiritual exercise. So, Mike and I sat comfortably on the edges of our beds or chairs after drying our bodies. We also settled in bed sometimes, but we often avoided our beds, to prevent us from falling asleep. Once we were adequately situated on the edges of our beds, chairs, or lying face-up in our beds, we were ready to exercise our minds. We stayed still and forgot about our immediate surroundings.

Mike often told me to imagine myself at my village or any location of my choice. He insisted that I take a mental picture of what was happening there as soon as I felt comfortable in the place. We often discussed the contents of my mental images after each exercise. Most times, he stopped me halfway and reminded me that my mind was synonymous with my brain. Mike loved to say that our thoughts were not in our chests or hearts and that what we referred to as incidents in our minds were usually reflections of what was happening in our brain. So, he insisted that it was my responsibility to keep my brain clear of negative thoughts. Also, Mike advised me to allow my spirit and soul to fill my mind with ideas of the good things I wanted. Halfway into the exercise one day, he asked, *"What do you want?"*

"To hit Bastards," I responded with a wry smile. The term *"Bastard"* was a derogatory name for members of opposing campus fraternities.

"Hitting is not necessary," Mike replied. *"We are victorious*

folks on campus, and no one dares us. What do you want?" He yelled.

"I want to go to my village" I replied.

"To do what?" he interjected.

"To get rid of that spot at the center of our family premises," I yelled back. *"I want to destroy those fetish objects at our family premises! I now believe in myself and can do anything I choose because I am in charge of myself!"* I shouted.

"Now, you are talking. You are a rugged man," Mike said, happily admonishing me to go back to my exercise.

About 15 minutes into our practice, he spoke gently into my ear. *"Go to your village in your mind and do what you said you would do. You have to do it first in the unseen realm before you do it physically. If anyone attempts to stop you, you can hit the person because hitting is allowed when you are doing good. Believe it and be fearless!"* he taught me.

Precisely 30 minutes later, we ended our exercise. According to Mike, the activity was meant to help us learn how to concentrate, set goals, and work on achieving them. It turned out that such exercises helped me chart my career path early in life to become a teacher. The quiet moments taught me how to concentrate while studying and how to reflect on what I had read afterward.

We also practiced feeling other people. We kept objects such as metal plates on a table in our room for about a week or so to make sure many people touched them. During our exercise, Mike and I would hold the plates to see if we could feel or get impressions about anyone who had come into contact with the dishes. Such a practice reminded me of Mr. Promise, our friend, who told me to disregard Mike and his philosophies because they were the products of excessive consumption of weed. I say so because I honestly did not understand what Mike wanted us to figure out by feeling other people's impressions.

Nevertheless, the most exciting part of my activities with Mike was that we avoided alcoholic drinks, smoking, or overeating about four days before any spiritual exercise. Also, we strove to be at peace with ourselves and with everyone around us. Mike insisted that quarreling and getting angry at anyone would disturb our connection with the unseen realm. Our spiritual exercises continued for many months until I headed home for the summer holiday. As I entered our family premises, I noticed the spot in the middle. I dashed to the area as if someone was chasing me. I kicked the spot with my left leg, scattering the structure.

All the wooden artifacts fell apart. I reached for each piece, put them together, and got kerosene from our kitchen. I poured the flammable liquid all over the items, retrieved a cigarette lighter from my pocket, and set the artifacts aflame. As the objects flickered in the blaze, I noticed that family members were watching me from afar. They would later tell me they thought I had gone mad. As the debris settled, I swept the place and poured the ashes into a bush behind our family house. I strolled out to smoke. After about an hour I returned, only to meet a furious uncle Bryan.

He told me that my actions confirmed to him that our family deity was angry at me. So, I was to stay back so he could call the native doctor who appeased the deity some years ago to do further spiritual work for me, or else the idol would destroy me. I apologized for ruining the place but was opposed to the idea of meeting a native doctor. He then said he was not surprised because he heard that I had joined a cult in college and also smoked marijuana. Parents and older folks in Nigeria liked to call fraternal organizations cults. He asserted that my demolition of what our family cherished and had preserved for many years had shown him that I was in the early stages of madness.

The following month, I went back to school. Mike and I worked hard to stay out of trouble. However, it seemed that the consequences of our previous actions were a fresh memory as we resolved to lead a trouble-free life. We had another fight with folks from a rival fraternity at a party on campus. The fight cut college short (again!), and a mob made up of angry students, chased us out of the school. Amidst the troubles, Mike left our room without informing me. He later sent word to me that anytime I heard fire on the mountain, I should not wait to hear *"Run, run, run."* Instead, I should run immediately. I moved to another school after about a year of hiatus because I had written the entrance exam shortly before the fight, as was now my habit.

Mike eventually enrolled for a part-time degree program at another college. I continued to believe in myself and engage in those exercises introduced to me by Mike. They calmed my nerves and helped me to focus on my studies. I later graduated from university with a combined honors degree in *Education and Political Science* while also working as an elementary school teacher. A year after college, I enrolled for a Masters' degree program in *International Relations and Strategic Studies*, which I juggled with teaching full-time at a high school. After completing my Masters, I registered for another graduate program in Journalism. Upon completion, I worked as a print journalist, college professor, and volunteer trainer for a nonprofit before pursuing further studies in Europe. I later relocated to the United States, where I earned a doctorate in education.

Meanwhile, I continued to believe in myself wholeheartedly, which worked just fine for me. I would later realize that belief in myself was an unconscious observance of the *Belief Literacy Steps*. The funny thing about belief is that, while nothing seems to have changed when you believe, believing activates something in you. Specifically, you will not taste, see, smell, touch, or hear any sound to signal a change upon believing, yet something has happened. Believing takes you beyond the senses and changes the way you see things.

If you stick to your beliefs long enough, your entire

life will change, whether for better or for worse. It does not matter what you believe. It could be in the efficacy of a piece of wood like a deity or any strange object, but they work the same. *Belief Literacy Steps* has shown me that some people revere such wooden idols merely because of their belief. Such people believed that those carved images would solve their problems, and their problems were solved eventually. As such, it helps to believe in something that is within your power to influence. For example, individuals who are healthy with sound minds may want to consider believing in themselves, which is also another way of putting your trust in something that resides inside you, but it is often a much higher phenomenon.

Self-belief will not work if you are someone who lacks guiding principles, such as a drug abuser, because you will hardly stick to plans. Drug abuse was the reason why my friends and I did silly things in college, which resulted in our inability to complete schooling in multiple universities.

Most times, those who believe in themselves end up learning that they have unknowingly relied on their source. In the following chapters, I will discuss some additional life lessons that cause me to juxtapose the behavior of some religious people to those of members of terrorist groups. I will share the experiences I garnered from learning and from teaching over the years. Also, I will show you how to steer your mind to greater heights in life merely by taking *Belief Literacy Steps*.

CHAPTER 7

Acts of Terror by Religious People

Terrorism comes in different shapes and forms because those who impose their ideas on others are guilty of ideological violence and intimidation.

My mom did not agree with the majority of my ideas. She believed that I attempted to understand spiritual things through human wisdom and evaluations based on knowledge acquired from Western education. She insisted that our senses were not enough for understanding the nature of God and His redemption plan through King Jesus Christ.

"Mom, I'm afraid I have to disagree with your reasoning about human wisdom," I told her. However, I agreed with her that the acquisition of Western education was not enough to enable one to understand spiritual things.

"What do you mean by that?" she asked.

I was saying that I had passed through Western

education up to a doctorate level, yet I remained nowhere closer to understanding spiritual stuff.

"Mom, could that be why Boko Haram terrorists are abducting schoolgirls in Northern Nigeria?" I heard that they want to put an end to Western education over there. Do you know that because of Boko Haram's incessant abduction of school kids, other school-age kids now prefer to stay at home?"

"What kind of education are they proposing?" She asked.

"I do not know the alternative education system they are offering, but I am sure I will not like it because of the violent nature of their ideology. They kill people with wanton disregard. There are legislative bodies in places where Boko Haram holds sway. I believe that individual members of Boko Haram can lobby lawmakers in their various constituencies to deliberate whatever they want in legislative houses." I replied.

"Boko Haram terrorists have better chances of accomplishing their objectives through lawmakers than through violence. I say so because force or violence does not work in Nigeria. Nothing has worked in Nigeria through the use of force or violence. Do you think I am exaggerating? I am not. Have you forgotten that many ethnic nationalities in Nigeria have used violent approaches to break away from Nigeria? Did any of such breakaway succeed? None of them were successful. In response, many successive Nigerian governments have used greater force and severe violence to address such issues. Sometimes, they use brutal force to bring straying ethnic groups back to the Nigerian polity."

The Igbos are a good example. They once broke away, but the Nigerian military forced them back into the Nigerian project after killing almost three million innocent people who did not play any role in the breakaway.

The Nigerian army has also massacred innocent people who protested the environmental degradation of their communities by multinational corporations that worked in concert with then repressive Nigerian governments. One may say that the military is no longer at the helm of Nigerian political administration, and are not able to quell the Boko Haram uprising. Such reasoning is flawed because one of the country's civilian presidents once used the military to raze down an entire community in the South southern zone of the country. Members of the community were accused of killing law enforcement officers. As a military that comprised of excellent professionals, they were known for quelling crises and acting as trailblazers. For example, the Nigerian army rallied members of the Economic Community of West African States (ECOWAS), and single-handedly intervened to save civilians in Liberia during the Liberian civil war. They were so confident in their might and capability that they did not wait on the then Organization of African Unity or the United Nations who were visibly dragging their feet.

As such, the delay by the Nigerian military and leaders of Nigerian political establishments to crush Boko Haram is, to say the least, surprising. How come the federal government has not unleashed the same terror they used in Southern Nigeria on Boko Haram operatives? Their lag and complicity notwithstanding, Boko Haram will not achieve its objectives in Nigeria through violence. I say so because there are unseen centrifugal and centripetal forces that hold Nigeria together. Violence does not sway those forces. It was in Northern Nigeria that people woke up one morning in 1999, and the governor of Zamfara state announced that he would break away from the English common law. He received overwhelming parliamentary support to make Sharia law the official legal system of Zamfara. He was smart because he did not employ violence. Shortly after, other states followed suit, and most states in Northern Nigeria are now using the Sharia legal system. They are also cohabiting with neighbors who are not using the Sharia law. I have taught at a college in Zamfara state. So, I know that Zamfara people are super friendly; with or without the Sharia law, they understand that violence is not a smart way of actualizing one's objectives.

I participated in a Nigerian youth service program in Zamfara state and saw firsthand how efficient their governance worked. Muslim security officers guarded non-Muslims in our camps to prevent fanatical Muslims from unleashing harm on non-Muslims. The governor gave campers extra food and money, which we called the *Bush* allowance. Campers participated in lots of community activities, and most times we joked about Christianity and Islam, but no one killed anyone. It is illegal to consume alcoholic drinks in the state, but as residents, we drank. It is not like in Dubai, where you receive some identification or license to purchase alcohol. We went to military bases to get drunk. We also drank alcohol at underground bars. Those bars were not inside the ground. They were in places disguised as grocery stores. After our drinking escapades, we took some more for the road. Some consumers of alcoholic beverages like to drink their one-for-the-road-drink before they leave. Others want to hit the road with one of their favorite drinks, but in Zamfara, we took many bottles for the way home. There were two reasons for this. First, such a grocery shop is not a place you want to visit often, so you have to maximize each visit. Finally, it is easy to conceal more than one drink in kettles. Because kettles served as water containers for ablution, anyone who saw you would assume that you were carrying water and heading for prayers at a mosque down the road.

I jokingly called my mom a terrorist because she was obsessed with the one-sided view of news coverage about terrorist activities prevalent in the mass media.

"How come almost all the terrorists they parade on television are members of the Islamic faith?" She once asked me.

"Momsy! We are thieves, but only the ones they catch and

parade on TV pass for thieves." I replied.

My mom failed to acknowledge that early Christian missionaries who came to Africa were terrorists. Those missionaries concealed their real intentions and vandalized many communities. In Africa, they stole cultural artifacts and natural resources. They were so terroristic they told natives that their way of life was barbaric, and their history was nothing but a dark age. To add salt to injury, they also said to them that the dark age was not a subject that was worthy of record. As such, the missionaries recorded the history of their victims and told them what to think. Some of their fellow Christians, who were part of the European business and political elite, sponsored slave ships and instigated communities to fight against themselves. A naïve onlooker would wonder why such men would incite communal wars but the reason is simple: whichever side that won would supply slaves to them. When Christian missionaries returned to their home country, the ruling elite would make them knights of the church.

These missionaries messed up the African psyche, which resulted in the suffering of future African generations. What is more terroristic than that? Indeed, religious people have given the world a dangerous dose of terrorism. I say so because terrorism comes in different shapes and forms, but it seems consistent that those who impose their ideas on others for the purpose of dismantling their psyche are also guilty of ideological violence and intimidation.

Perplexed by my description of her religious affiliation as terroristic, she asked,

"Do you not know that Nigeria is a religious irony?"

"Why do you say so?" I asked.

"Can you talk about Nigeria without mentioning the havoc Muslim Fulani nomadic cattle herders are wreaking every day in the country?" she queried.

"I am aware that those herders have given Nigeria her gravest security threat as they seem to have killed more Nigerians than Boko Haram." I replied.

"Mum," I added, *"No matter the angle from which you look at terrorism in Nigeria, you will see that Christians and Muslims have contributed their ignoble share to put that beautiful country on the map of terrorist countries."*

CHAPTER 8
Beliefs of Select Fraternal Organizations

I know all the things I know, but I do not know all the things that know me.

Studying in multiple countries and meeting people from various cultural backgrounds helped me to reflect on belief objectively. I understood that all the things Mike and I sought back in college from small cities and villages in West Africa were universal human needs. Your exact place of residence or where you were born does not matter. Human beings share common fundamental needs and values. From areas such as Abuja to Abu Dhabi, Brisbane to Barcelona, Buenos Aires to Beijing, Cairo to Calgary, Chennai to Copenhagen, or Denver to Diriamba, everyone wants a better life. There are more existing factors that unite people than those that endure to divide them. Even the lonely scientists at research stations in Antarctica share the same ideals as their colleagues in luxurious laboratories located in wealthy cities like Chicago and Osaka.

Armed with such knowledge, I returned home one autumn holiday to search for my buddy, Mike. I met Micro somewhere in Port Harcourt, the Garden City of Nigeria. I explained to him how I traveled to many countries across four continents and had noticed that the funny ideas we had cultivated in college were universal. Out of an overabundance of curiosity, which attracted us to each other years ago, we agreed to learn more about other things people believed and their reasons for these beliefs. We grew up in homes where beliefs in the Christian and Islamic faiths held sway. However, the behavior of adherents of those religions were boring to Mike and I. My mom, who went from being a Christian to a born-again Christian is an example. In my opinion, she and other born-agains misunderstand the biblical injunction that one has to be born again to enter God's kingdom. Being born again should be about changing the way you think, confessing Christ as Lord, and becoming a new person at heart. I do not believe that being born again is a title to attach to your name. Once your thinking is changed because of this rebirth, your behavior will reflect the change. My mom disagreed. She almost wore a name tag to display her progression from Christianity to Bornagain-ism. *"What happened to being transformed by the renewal of your mind?"* I often asked her.

I also reminded Mike about Ali, our close pal with whom we often went to the mosque. From being a Muslim,

Ali became a super strict Muslim who engaged in elaborate prayers, fasting, and adopted a dress code to flaunt the Islamic faith. He grew eloquent in public speaking and would act as the mouthpiece of all Muslims, whereas his lifestyle contradicted the ideas he expounded.

He went as far as saying that he supported the killing of fellow Muslims, whom he tagged unbelievers. The so-called unbelievers were Muslims who did not subscribe to *his* beliefs. He insisted that it was permissible to shed their blood and, if possible, take their wealth. Simple things that didn't matter to him in the past became issues of concern. Suddenly, each morning, Ali would ask: "Guys, which side of this room is facing east?" so that he would know where to face while praying. Mike often replied to him by yelling: "Ask your geography teacher."

Most times, I would add, *"And do not call us infidels."*

I agreed with Ali about the need to obey the Quranic injunction to face the sacred mosque. However, the Quran also noted that where you face will not be counted for you as righteousness. Some Muslims make it an issue, and when you disagree with them, they see you as an *unbeliever.* So, Mike and I decided not to look at belief from the viewpoint of practitioners of Christianity or Islam, as we had had enough. We agreed to explore beliefs from individuals who people perceived as members of secret societies because their lives were often shrouded in secrecy. We decided to visit one of my uncles, who was tagged a secret society member while we were growing up.

My uncle was a tenured professor at a first-generation university in Nigeria. He welcomed us into his office and hosted us lavishly. However, he swore on his life that he did not belong to any secret society. I reminded him that I had seen paraphernalia of Ailism, Pruyiaism, Sonism, and Qanianism in his house. Moreover, they were the four organizations everyone at home believed were the secret societies to which he belonged while we were growing up.

"How did you know the names of those organizations?" he asked, shocked. I explained to him how I and my cousin Kinky, his son, had been secretly reading materials from his library. Also, for over ten years, Kinky and I had the spare key to his private study, where he never allowed anyone to enter, including his wife. He proceeded to give Mike and I a long lecture about the universe and how curiosity killed the cat. Finally, he said those organizations had secrets, but they were not *secret societies*. As we stepped out of his office, I told Mike that my uncle forgot to point out that satisfaction brought back the cat. As such, I suggested to Mike that we should ask more people. Mike looked at me and said that anyone who did not come would not know. I understood him. During our college days, many people misunderstood our frat activities. So, we used that phrase to indicate that no one could ever know what we did without becoming a part of it.

What Mike meant was that we needed to join those

organizations in order to understand their activities. My uncle was a smart man, but he must have forgotten that we share similar genes, and that I never gave up. I was surprised that he thought I would walk away satisfied with such a vague answer. His answer was a joke. It was a blatant play on words, but I was unwilling to forgive the pun. A dictionary will tell you that a *secret society* is a group of people or association that hides some of its activities from nonmembers. I nodded at Mike's suggestion. I knew Mike. He was a zillion times more determined than I was; once his mind was made up, nothing could stop him. Of the four organizations, we decided to begin with Ailism. I reached out to my uncle's friend, who signed advertorials in newspapers for public lectures of Ailism. He was happy to hear that my friend and I were seeking the truth.

So, he quickly gave us the drill:

"Buy and read the three volumes of the book entitled *Knowing Ailism*." After that, he continued, "I will connect you to a panel of people who will interview you to determine your readiness to seek the luminous height. If you sail through, you will participate in an initiatory process that will make you a bearer of the light."

That was easy. Knowing me as a voracious reader, Mike delegated me to get the three books and do the reading. I went to the office of my uncle's friend six days later and requested to meet the panel. Happy that I had read the three books that quickly, he told me that I had a light spirit and would ascend fast if I continued to seek the truth with such pace. The following weekend, we assembled at the center of Ailism in our city, as planned. We met other seekers, and all of us went into a room for a review of the books I had read. Halfway into the discussion, I disagreed with the instructor when he insisted that the resurrection of Jesus Christ did not happen physically according to the revelations given to the author of the books I read. He cited gravity as something that would have pushed Jesus down, and I mentioned aerodynamics as something that could keep him afloat. I suggested that he balance his analysis.

While I was not holding a brief for Christianity, I remembered that my mom had always told me that the resurrection is the core of Christian faith. My mom knew I loved to read books, and I had works containing mystical and esoteric teachings. So, any opportunity she had, she would remind me that I should detest any knowledge that counters the resurrection. I demanded to know from the instructor how such knowledge was revealed to the author while history recorded something different. He concluded that I was not ready for the initiation and rescheduled our appointment. Mike was not happy with me. He explained to me that we were on a mission and that our mission was not to disagree with anyone or disclose what my mother taught me.

"My brother, you screwed it up," Mike whispered into my ear, angrily. I apologized profusely, but I knew that once he was angry, nothing could make him change his mind. That explains why I called him a short man with tall anger. He told me to consider our adventure with Ailism as inconclusive, like elections in Nigeria.

For the remaining three organizations, Mike suggested that we ignore Pruyiaism, because it does not have global membership, and split the other two between us. I should go for one while he goes for the other. So, he chose to explore Sonism. Today, you can request for membership online, but those days, association with Sonism was through word of mouth and introduction. You needed a member to petition for you to join. So, Mike faced two problems: locating a member who would also be willing to request membership for him. Eventually, one of our schoolmates introduced him to someone who linked him up with a member of Sonism. The man agreed to petition for Mike but told us that he had not paid his membership dues for a couple of years. As such, he would be unable to request membership for anyone until he was financially up to date. I told Mike that we would give the man money to pay up, and after a short time, he would petition for Mike. I offered to pay for Mike but before I could send money, I needed to go back to Europe to receive my school allowance. My father would kill me if I cashed my school money in Nigeria. So, I left for Europe the following week. Two weeks later, I sent money home for the payment. After about three months, the man facilitated Mike's membership.

Compared to what Mike passed through, it seemed that the process for joining Qanianism would be simple. They advertised their organization through mass media and encouraged people to explore membership, but there was no guarantee of admission. Besides that, Mike and I followed the celebrated rift of a church and Qanianism closely. For almost 20 years, a church ruffled the judicial system. This church sought the proscription of Qanianism because they believed Qanianism to be a secret society. The case reached the supreme court of their country of operation and was eventually struck out as bizarre. So, I told Mike that those people were not a secret society according to the precedent set by that ruling. Mike became furious. "Where is your learner's permit? Are you now learning how frats work?" he yelled at me. "Do you not know that no court can label any organization a secret society?" Mike took me down memory lane and reminded me that secret societies were often made up of smart people who understood how legal processes worked. As such, Mike considered it strange that a church hoped they would win the case.

"It could be possible that those judges are members of one secret society or the other," he continued. "There are things you know to be accurate but cannot prove in court." Finally, he drove home his point by reminding me how some of our former schoolmates registered many proscribed campus frats outside college with different names.

Some of those organizations are thriving legal entities around the world, known by the unsuspecting public as social clubs, nonprofits, religious, and educational organizations. He also reminded me how members of such organizations engaged in philanthropy and participated in political activities to control societal affairs.

"Can anyone be ignorant enough to accuse them of being secret societies?" he questioned.

"Nope," I replied.

Mike encouraged me to ignore the reasoning of the supreme court and proceed with my application so we could figure things out for ourselves. I applied for membership, and they accepted me. By the time I became a part of the elementary degree stage, Mike had become an aspirational master. Because we chose to study their degrees, I realized that both organizations involved lots of reading. However, Qanianism entailed more reading than Sonism. We continued for more than ten years and reached their most advanced degrees.

We got to where their differences shrunk, and similarities became apparent. Like my uncle, I did not label them a secret society or even an occultic group. I felt stupid when I reached the same conclusion as my uncle. However, I was happy because I encountered many things my uncle did not tell me. Such organizations were better understood when you experienced them because most of their guiding principles are unwritten. For example, how can you explain the idea that you cannot find the truth on pages of paper? How can you deal with the perception that a teacher will appear only when a student is ready?

Unfortunately, such teachings were structured in degrees that conditioned your mind to poke holes into everything you learned at Sunday school. There is also the appearance of a vicious attack on the kingship of Jesus Christ. The teachings of their degrees reduced Jesus to just a highly incarnated architect, master, or teacher, unlike the King and Lord He is. They are also hesitant to acknowledge that no one can see God except through Jesus Christ. Additionally, I understood that the difference between Ailism and these other organizations was timing. Ailism was quick to attack the fundamental teachings of Jesus Christ in the first three volumes of their introductory book.

The other organizations encouraged adherents to identify with their faith in any established religion of their choice. However, as you continue to study the philosophies of their degrees, you will start to view all religious beliefs as one. Are all faiths indeed one? They also preach religious tolerance, which is a smokescreen to hide their real message. Gradually, they shift the nature of God from what your mom, dad, or grandparents taught you at the dinner table. God suddenly becomes a mere architect who designed the world, supreme intelligence who lives in your head, or something in your emotions. You begin to revere visible and invisible masters, who are or were ordinary humans like you, but have been or are going through a series of evolution. Do you remember uncle Bryan and his ancestral worship? Those people he names during the April ceremony can pass for his past masters, but conventional wisdom ridicules him because he did not structure his knowledge in degrees. Remember my fans and cheerleaders? They were my invisible masters who guided my steps.

Conventional wisdom forgets that uncle Bryan is from an oral tradition where to date, essential secrets are not written anywhere but passed orally from person to person. These organizations also preach the illusory brotherhood of man. Mike was shocked when he attended their functions in the United States.

"If there is a genuine universal brotherhood of man, why do they have lodges that are exclusively for Black people and others solely for White people?" he asked as we drove from Lincoln to Minneapolis. They put it in writing that any of their members could join any lodge of his choice, but in reality, some lodges accept people of specific color because of their independent nature. Some lodges are also for the rich and mighty, whereas some are for the poor and ordinary folks. Unlike Sonism, I give Qanianism some credit for practicing genuine brotherhood. While their lodges were also independent like Sonism, affiliation is open to all members regardless of color or race. Qanianism is even more in tune with the time than Sonism because they accept men and women who are pursuing personal luminescence.

Notwithstanding, I believe that one is better off a lone ranger than joining fraternal organizations due to the advantages of the internet and social media. You can make friends and build relationships that will stand the test of time over the internet. Without any doubt, most people will agree that the Internet has changed our lives in immeasurable ways. For example, many years ago, we walked into stores to buy things. Today, you can make purchases with the touch of a button or the utterance of a few words to an app. You pay by punching in some numbers from a plastic card issued by a bank, and you receive what you ordered within a short time. Online stores can even use drones to carry your items to your location if you are in a hurry. As such, the world wide web can help people to develop genuine fraternal relationships, whether we realize it or not.

CHAPTER 9

Believing the Knowledgeable and Exploiting the Believers

Most of what we perceive through our senses build our beliefs.

I was at my doctor's office in West Houston one afternoon in October of thirteen years ago. He told me that there was a possibility that I would die in ten years if I did not quit smoking.

"Should I write in your file that I am treating a smoker or nonsmoker?"

His question frightened and perplexed me. After a long pause, I said "nonsmoker." I later walked out of his office, and to date, I have not smoked anything, including inhaling second-hand smoke. Like a plague, I avoid places that may expose me to smokers. My doctor said a couple of things about high blood pressure, kidney disease, and smoking. He explained how high blood pressure could block vessels that supply blood to the kidney. According to him, such action can prevent the removal of fluids and raise blood pressure. He also said that my blood pressure could reach a dangerous level and lead to a heart attack, which may, in return, cause death. I did not know precisely how he arrived at such a conclusion. I did not even understand half of what he said, but I knew I did not want to die. So, I believed him instantly because of the fear of death.

I got home in Southwest Houston, still shaking as if death was chasing me.

"Are you okay?" my brother asked. I told him what happened. He almost passed out laughing at me.

"Stop shaking, you will not die," he said to me. "If smoking kills, I would have died many years before your birth." My brother is a chain smoker, but that was not enough reason to believe him.

"Why do you believe that smoking cannot kill me?" I asked.

"Because I have smoked for over 30 years without any plan to quit," he replied. "I am a living example that smoking does not kill," he continued. "It is all in your mind; if you believe that smoking will kill you, then you will die from smoking."

"Thanks for your advice, big brother, but I am not smoking anymore," I said, resolute. I left for my room with the resolve not to return to smoking. Apart from the fear of death, I also believed my doctor because of his training in medicine. I did not believe my brother because he was an electrical engineer and an active smoker. I did not regard my brother as someone knowledgeable in medicine or human anatomy.

Similarly, I witnessed a doctor in Chinese medicine burning herbs around acupuncture needles stuck on the back of my friend.

"Why do you use those herbs and needles?" I asked him.

"These herbs will help your friend's body to restore itself," he replied. "That is what we believe in Chinese medicine, and it works," he clarified. I also believed him instantly without probing if he was right or wrong in his assessment. On many different occasions, I have asked the same question to Japanese and Korean people who use herbs for medicinal purposes. All of them pointed to a long-held system or systems of belief to explain why they continued to use herbs. I also asked traditional medicine men known as herbalists in many African countries, and they gave the same reply. Because they are medical practitioners knowledgeable in various fields of medicine, I had no other alternative but to believe them.

Over twenty years after I witnessed our family's April ceremony, I asked uncle Bryan why he continues to be interested in the event. Smiling, he narrated to me what his father and grandfather told him more than 80 years ago. They said that the ceremony exemplified an ancestral belief in our people.

"It is our custom and the source of what has guided our people for thousands of years. In short, that is how we talk to God, and that is why I believe in the ceremony," he concluded.

To believe is a vital aspect of being human. You are a believer when you think through something and accept the thing as being accurate and correct. Sometimes, some people recognize and believe what other people have thought without asking questions. I call such people blind believers. Also in existence are some people who do not believe. Lacking belief is tantamount to not admitting that something is accurate and correct. As such, I consider those who lack a sense of belief as also following some form of belief system because they or someone else have thought through their conclusions for them.

There are many things we believe. Those things are either improving our lives or limiting us from reaching new heights. For example, the United States is the most powerful country on Earth, and Americans agree that all men are created equal, yet Americans discriminate among themselves along racial lines. Might and power notwithstanding, racism is the most significant fault line of American life. Human beings also use what their fellow humans believe in enslaving one another because belief is a potent weapon. Many people have fallen victim to what they believe at one point or the other, including the high, low, rich, poor, educated, and uneducated. As noted earlier in this paragraph, people who live in the United States experience it first-hand. A fundamental belief in the U.S. is that human beings are bequeathed with equal rights by their creator. As such, those who seek political offices ride on such belief and promise to create avenues for fair treatment of every minority if elected. Unfortunately, many Americans would not agree that they receive the same procedure in treatment as others.

Evidence of massive inequality in income and access to opportunities abounds in the U.S. Moreover, Americans who belong to minority groups sometimes work harder than mainstream folks, yet they only get halfway on the road to the equal rights they believe are inherent in their lives. Conversely, some Americans who are in the minority play the race card due to their belief system. Sometimes, they shout foul where none exist or when they err instead of acknowledging their faults. For example, some people exploit racism in order to advance ulterior motives. Such people believe that playing the race card will attract attention and blow things out of proportion to their advantage. Periodically, they succeed because racism is alive and thriving in the United States. Indeed, people who are in racial minorities talk about how others discriminate against them while members of racial majority insist that discrimination has flip-flopped as others now discriminate against *them*.

Nigeria offers another example of how people exploit

others because of what they believe. The average Nigerian has a different understanding of the same concept than the Nigerian political elite. For example, both of them agree that the government should control all natural resources in the country. They also agree that land is a natural resource. However, in some parts of Nigeria, people sell their lands and pay appropriate taxes to the government. In other parts of the country, people are not allowed to do the same because their area has crude oil underneath. If you mine the oil in your backyard within your property, the government will call it "bunkering." They call it "refining" when the government uses pipes to siphon the oil in someone's backyard to faraway places where they export the oil. Meanwhile, that siphoning and selling process means that appropriate infrastructure is put in place at the point of sale using the oil money. By extension, they develop the areas where they sell the oil while the source of the oil is in infrastructural shambles.

The divergence in understanding of ownership and management of natural resources emanates from the fact that the government attaches more value to resources in some places in the country than in other places. Lands in areas with more natural resources are valuable in the eyes of the government, which prompts the government to deviate from a collectively agreed meaning and understanding. As such, the Nigerian government and members of its political elite humiliate and abuse ordinary people in order to extract their natural resources. Funnily enough, the only crime such people committed is that they were born in places with large deposits of natural resources. The few Nigerians who constitute the political elites of the country also preach the need for a majority of Nigerians to tighten their belts. Such political power brokers profess a belief that the Nigerian economy is not functioning as expected. Thus, so many Nigerians live in abject poverty while yearning or hoping for a better future.

In spite of what they cause their countrymen to think and believe, those power brokers move Nigerian wealth around the world for their selfish ends. Such Nigerians are constant players on the playgrounds of the famous, high, mighty, and rich in many countries. They rub shoulders with those who matter in other parts of the world. As a student in Europe, I saw many Nigerians who flew into European countries on weekends to attend nightclubs. They would return to Nigeria on Sunday evenings to re-sume their regular weekly activities. For such people, their workweek runs from Monday to Thursday. They dedicate the rest of their week to gallivanting and high-end fun. They institute guidelines they themselves do not intend to adhere to, yet other Nigerians believe them because of the *power of belief*. Those power brokers often introduce and implement structural adjustment programs. Such programs force many Nigerians to reduce their consumption level while the power brokers are busy vacationing overseas and enlarging their economic coast. Also, all Nigerians believe that Nigerian roads and airspace are for collective use. Thus, they expect everyone to share them. The rich have a different belief. They share the roads with others, but the airspace they keep for themselves. During heavy traffic on roadways or when they have doctor's appointments, they make phone calls and have private jets pick them out of the traffic, leaving the roads for the poor.

The tendency to behave in a manner that depicts what people believe is not restricted to the rich and mighty, as poor people are also complicit. Many Nigerians who are financially destitute and uneducated sell their votes during public elections, because of their belief in instant gratification. As such people queue in line to cast their ballots during elections, they go for the highest bidder among the agents of those seeking political offices. They accept money and cast their votes in favor of those who pay a larger sum. Because most elective positions in Nigeria have four-year tenure, it is comical how such adherents of instant gratification spend four years raining blames on those who bought their votes, because the vote buyers use their entire office time to amass wealth in enormous proportion. Unfortunately, they repeat such electoral behavior every four years. Both the vote sellers and vote buyers continue in the cycle because of their belief system.

The belief in taking a shortcut reminds me of the similarities between Nigeria and the United States. Both countries have citizens who believe that their children should not follow set standards to gain admission to elite universities. As such, they pay their way through with the help of fraudulent officials who manipulate university entrance procedures. In the U.S., crooked consultants and sports coaches do the dirty work while in Nigeria, professional examination writers and dishonest school officials facilitate the shortcuts.

Around the world, I have spoken with men who said they believed that life was all about obtaining beautiful women, nice cars, and fancy clothes. Such men declared that they regularly engage in activities that will help them to fulfill the objectives of their beliefs. Some of these men acknowledged a belief in the propitiation of spirits and engagement in rituals for material wealth. One such ceremony includes human sacrifice, which may sound odd to an outsider. However, lessons from the Maya culture have taught us so much about human sacrifice. We have also heard of mass child sacrifice in Peru. In so-called civilized societies, some women believe it is okay to become pregnant without any intention to carry the fetus to term. Such women end up aborting the fetus on the altar of convenience and pleasure due to the belief that they own their bodies and can do as they wish.

In contrast, other women use what they believe in criticizing those who think they own their bodies. The other women insist that their bodies are like facilities they hold on trust for the one who created women and gave them the capacity to conceive and bear children. They posit that human bodies are temples where the creator lives. Thus, they believe that women should not conceive and abort pregnancies at will.

I have also spoken with countless fraudsters who informed me that they participated in fraudulent activities because of what they believed. The cheats nurture a strong belief that the proceeds they get from fraud are resources that were stolen from their forefathers by the forefathers of the individuals they choose to defraud. As nefarious as that may sound, it is an indication that human beings often do what they do because of what they believe. Some men also engage in sexual violence against underage girls because of their belief that such an act cures sexually transmitted infections. I have heard about how men perpetrate such acts in many places in Africa and Europe, but contrary to their opinion, those men only succeed in spreading diseases.

An uncle of my friend, from a country in East Africa, was murdered by members of a neighboring community who stole children in plain sight. Weird as it may sound, these child-thieves believe that child abduction is the only way they can become parents because they are not able to procreate. Unlike what the uninformed may conclude, all the stolen children are not always put up as domestic or sex slaves. Some of the abducted children who are up to 16 years of age are forced into early marriage, while younger ones become a part of the family of their abductors. Unfortunately, most of the children die as a result of the trauma they experience by being forced off of their parents. Similar things have also happened in places like Chicago in the United States, where a woman strangled another woman, so she could remove the baby in the womb of the strangled woman and pretend that the baby was hers. Such an act shows that human beings are capable of engaging in activities that even defy one's imagination and rationality because of their belief systems. However, I believe that such individuals are operating from a psychotic state of mind.

Saudi Arabia offers a positive example of human activities based on belief. A newly crowned prince takes over the reins of power. He empowers women, against age-old norms, because of what he believes, and a new normal is born. Similarly, an emperor abdicates power to usher in an era of order and harmony in Japan. While wishing peace to the world, he cited age and declining health as reasons for giving up power. However, his real motives were his beliefs. In an era where Arab Spring has to unseat leaders, it helps to see that positive ideas still propel some men.

Belief systems unite and regulate people's behavior. An appropriate belief system leads to better decisions. Indeed, knowing what you believe simplifies your life because we waste time and energy acting in ways that are inconsistent with our beliefs. Having a common belief helps people to share a common destiny. What we believe results from what we are thinking, have thought, or what someone else has thought through a part of the human body we know as the brain. Our behavior represents our beliefs. So, the most significant way we can control our lives is to control our thoughts. Our thoughts reflect everything about us. As a result, people who succeed in managing their thoughts will do the most catastrophic evil or the most paramount good in life. Will the knowledge that your destiny is a product of your thinking cause you to unthink your thoughts?

CHAPTER 10

Reasoning Behind Our Actions

Shouldn't those who believe they evolved from apes reach out to their ape-ancestors for help?

Something motivates everything we do in life. This motive or reason for our actions subtly shows up in what we have done. Our motivation might be something we hide in our minds or a bunch of words written down on something elsewhere. Also, our activities can represent reactions to someone else's motive, but there is always a reason or reasons for our actions. We may not want to acknowledge this, but if we follow each other long enough, we will notice that our works display hints that can lead to the reasons why we act the way we do. Additionally, our steps manifest our beliefs. However, I have seen that the quickest way to know why someone is doing or has done something is to ask the person. As such, I decided to ask people to tell me the *why* behind their actions. I have had the privilege of asking lots of people to describe the reasoning behind their actions for me.

"Why did the United States and other major powers record many more positives to the COVID-19 pandemic after China?" I asked Anderson, a good friend of mine.

"It centers on a certain belief system. Political office holders in your so-called major powers have embraced a dangerous version of nationalism. When the virus was in its early stages in Wuhan, China, officials of these countries considered it to be a foreign disease. Some even termed it The Chinese Disease, showing they viewed COVID-19 as a distant phenomenon. China was merely a faraway country," he explained to me.

"What do you mean?" I queried.

"Some of these countries closed their borders to mirror their anti-globalization type of nationalism. However, what they failed to understand was that viruses do not see barriers, borders, or national boundaries in the transmission process," he elaborated.

"What should they have done?" I continued.

"It is simple. They should have sent help to China and worked with Chinese authorities to contain the outbreak. I remember how a previous U.S. administration under Obama sent experts to Sierra Leone during the outbreak of Ebola. No matter what you believe, one thing is undeniable: we need each other," Anderson concluded.

I asked a childhood friend of mine about her reasons

for becoming a lesbian. I was curious because she and I were friends during our teenage years, so I knew her as being straight. She smiled and gave me a litany of sad stories about men, which included me.

"Which woman wants to be with a man when there is a loving woman or a sex toy to satisfy her?" she asked, rhetorically.

"Tina," I said, "we have come a long way, and I witnessed your marriage to Bongo after we graduated from college, so please, tell me what prompted you to become a lesbian."

She responded, "I know that I have not been a lesbian my whole life. I became a lesbian at some point in my life due to a medical condition I do not want to disclose here, the medical issue has prevented me from being a wife in the traditional sense. I have known and befriended many lesbians. The problem has been that people thought I was weird. You know how folks from my tribe in Africa perceive lesbianism. No member of my family accepted the fact that I do not have any desire or emotional longing for any man. During the time I was a senior in high school, I mentioned it to my mother. She later told my father, and it earned me the spanking of my life. As a lesbian, I have never been accepted by anyone in my family even though I get along well with guys. So, after college, I married your friend. With him, I confirmed that guys would never fulfill my desires in spite of the fact that we got along very well. Also, I confirmed that men were not willing to accept my medical condition.

Before the marriage, I was in and out of ugly relationships with guys, and I wouldn't say I liked that. While I was married, I spent time doing other things to avoid having sex with him. I must admit that he was a kind, loving person who did many good things for me. However, I felt pressured to engage in sexual intercourse with him, but I wasn't strong enough to say no. Besides that, I did not want to embarrass myself and my parents by running away from my marriage. Divorce was a taboo topic, so it was not an option. Yes, even while married to him, I always admired other women. I know about many women who shared similar circumstances with me, but there was little to nothing any of us could do."

She continued, "My options were limited back then until I traveled overseas for graduate studies, and a new world opened for me. I met lots of females who viewed sexuality from a lens that was similar to mine. I got close to one; she was beautiful and a super sweet woman. Before I knew it, one thing naturally progressed to another, and as I speak, we are happily married. I went into a relationship with her while still married to your friend. At that point, my head was no longer with the man I called my husband. My head always wandered, yearning for the loving female I now call the love of my life. Within a few months of such, I decided to stop trying to be someone else. I had to live my life and be happy no matter what I lost. My parents disowned me, but it may shock you to hear that I did everything within my power to help them see reasons to accept me as a part of their family to no avail. At this time, I am out and proud of who I am. My sweetheart is awesome. My baby makes me happier than anyone in the world," she concluded.

In another instance, I asked one of my brothers to tell me how he went from being gay, well known to family members, to getting married to a woman and leading a completely different lifestyle. "I believe it was due to peer pressure. While attending high school at an all-boys seminary, I joined my school mates to practice homosexuality. I can say that peer pressure pushed me into a promiscuous gay lifestyle, which continued for many years, but I am glad that my parents sent me for counseling, and the rest is now history. I am happily married to a woman, and we have three kids. I believe that the global gay rights movement, which I joined in college, helped blind my eyes to my foolishness. The ideology of the movement abused and damaged my psyche. I should not have identified with them."

I once asked my mom to tell me how she would feel if I told her I was gay.

"Gay? God forbid, I would kill myself for you," she said, circling her right hand across her head.

"What would happen if you visited me and saw that I was married to Charlie, my childhood friend?" I inquired.

Instead of answering my questions, she walked away from the living room. My mom is one of those people who makes you question whether or not we should rely on our ideas. She is rigid and out of touch with the times. She would rather drive to a post office to send a letter to me instead of quickly emailing me. I believe that human society is evolving. As such, we should grow and keep pace with the changing times. There are many changes in our social structure, which have shifted the meanings we use to attach to things such as marriage and its impact on the family. How about allowing people to practice any sexual orientation of their choice?

My parents raised me at a time when parents consisted of a male whom my siblings and I called father, and a female, whom we called mother. I know my grandparents. They were also a male and a female. As I raise my children in the 21st century, I have passed on our family's understanding of marriage to them. My children consider marriage as something that happens between a male and a female. We have talked about when my daughters will start having boyfriends. My sons are also aware of the right time for them to begin to have girlfriends. We have a tacit understanding in our home that someday, they will get married to people of the opposite sex. However, my wife and I live with our kids next to two lovely ladies who are married and also raising a daughter. Two houses away on our right-hand side live two men who are also the parents of a little boy.

How do I teach my children that the meaning of marriage has evolved? How will my children reconcile the fact that a male and a female constitute parents for them, unlike our neighbors? Sometimes when our neighbor's children come over to play with mine, I overhear them talk about their parents. Funnily enough, all of the children see their parentage as a usual thing. One day my youngest child referred to our neighbor's parents as the *modern parents.*

"What do you mean by that?" I asked.

"They are modern because they have all male and all female parents," she explained.

"We are also modern," I lied, with a wry smile. Due to my confidence in the capability of the brain, an exceptional feature of the human body, to help me understand how to handle such an issue with my children, I put on my thinking cap. I realized that I might be neglecting my children if I fail to discuss such an issue with them. I may also be deceiving them if I insist that marriage is only for a male and a female. Ultimately, I may be failing in my fatherly role if I refuse to tell my children to view same sex couples as legally married if they are in places like our state where such union is legal.

Be that as it may, my thinking seems to have failed me because my mind has more questions than answers. My gay neighbors and I have a good relationship, so I am not worried about interacting with them daily. I only hope that their children and mine do not get confused about what constitutes parentage. My other neighbors are concerned about children who are cross-dressing at school, not what is happening in our own neighborhood. According to one of them, her six-year-old son is disturbed by classmates cross-dressing at our local elementary. The craziest part is that the school expects other kids to allow the cross-dressing pupils to call the shots on how to address them. As such, they can be boys on a Tuesday and decide to have others see them as girls on Wednesday.

"How is that a problem?" I asked one of my neighbors who was concerned, and she exploded.

"Last week, my son referred to his classmate as a boy. Today, he talked about the same classmate as a girl. It is affecting my son. Besides that, should we even allow a bunch of kids in primary school to cross-dress? I may have to start homeschooling my child after discussing with his father," she retorted.

I thought about what my neighbor said, but could not contribute anything to assuage her fears. My brain seemed to have failed me again, I mused to myself as I walked back to my home.

I continued to mull everything over in my mind. Why are two males partnering to raise children? Why are two females okay with raising children without any input from a male? These four neighbors of mine whom I have known for a long time, are from families that comprised a male as a father and a female as a mother. They grew up knowing their fathers and mothers as I did.

I have seen instances in Africa where women married women for procreation. However, such women relied on men to have kids and their children knew both women as mothers. Indeed, mom has been a woman and dad a man. Could such a weird arrangement be a product of evolution? Perhaps, we are evolving. I remember learning about how species develop in my high school biology classrooms. I learned that some characteristics of individual species use the process of natural selection to change over several generations. Behaviors such as the one causing my neighbor's concern could be due to changes from our phenotype interacting with different kinds of environments. Could that be the reasoning behind all that?

Evolution is a topic that fascinates me because I believe in the possibility that human beings may have evolved their way to where they are at the moment. So, I sat for long hours, ruminating on how we changed. *How would our ape-like predecessors have felt if they were alive today and noticed that we are marrying people of the same sex? Happy, of course! They will be like, "You higher animals are latecomers, we have been engaging in homosexual activities since like, forever."* Unfortunately, such a response would not answer all my questions. If we evolved from higher apes, it probably would not be wrong to expect some answers from our forbears. Has evolution answered the questions bordering on the delay for all primates to evolve into humans? In the absence of help from our source, I wonder if we are evolving or have reached the peak of our development. Won't there be any more evolution? How about evolutionary forces? Are they not capable of controlling our behaviors?

I also thought about God. He (or She) could be something human beings created from the depths of their conscious mind, out of fear of the unknown, and suggested to their subconscious mind. For example, some people who live in riverine or coastal areas attribute most of what they term "Gods" to sources they trace to rivers, seas, and oceans. I have also seen people who show honor and reverence for huge trees, which they consider gods. Others worship their dead relatives and refer to them as gods. Most religious people insist that God created us. If God created us, should we not have some expectations of God? Shouldn't God give us answers to the many questions that plague our lives daily? Those who profess that God created us also insist that we should believe in God rather than on things we can influence, such as our minds.

Why should we even believe in God? Why should we accept that God created humanity? Does that not make humans helpless? Are humans under the whims and caprice of this aforementioned God? Are we too frail to control ourselves? It is much easier to believe in science than in a God you can't see. I say so because science has thrown light on most of the issues that confront our daily lives.

Because of science, we are better human beings today than we were 100 years ago.

For example, we have increased life expectancy due to advances in medical sciences. Wait a minute, does science honestly answer all our questions about life? My friend, an atheist, answered in the affirmative. She agrees that science has solved all our problems. As such, she discourages people from praying to God. She believes that prayer works, but not for the same reason as a person who claims to be Christian, Hindu, Muslim, or a member of any religious group. According to my friend, "Prayer is useful because your brain, not God, answers prayer. As you make requests through what you call prayer, you condition your brain or mind to go to work in fulfilling your request — putting yourself together to pray causes you to concentrate and unconsciously think up solutions to the problem that prompted you to pray initially. You activate your subconscious mind to come up with a solution quickly. The act of praying helps you to see favorable circumstances that were already there, but you did not see them before then because your mind was not together. It is like bringing everything in you to work with your brain to provide solutions to your problems," she affirms. Is that enough reason to ascribe an almighty status to science?

In the summer of 2005, one of my students took his life. Ten years later, someone gunned down another one of my students. Each time I remember my late students,

I remember that most countries talk more about societal problems like suicide, gun violence, and school gun violence when they happen. When the news dies down, people go back to living life, as usual, believing that it will not happen again. There are more things I recall that make me skeptical about the power of the sciences. Humanity witnessed a devastating earthquake in the Indian Ocean on the eve of the mid-2000s. I remember the accompanying tsunami as if it were yesterday for several reasons. First, my cousin and his family were among the thousands who perished in the aftermath of the unpleasant event. Secondly, such natural disasters make me wonder about the fallibility of the human brain. I believe that human beings may not be able to stop earthquakes and tsunamis, but they can initiate and implement actions to reduce the impact of such calamities. Such reduction efforts should begin from research to safety education and building effective warning systems. We should also understand the importance of erecting safe structures as well as ways to avoid human-induced disasters. Humans should prepare for such emergencies to ensure we have an adequate mechanism in place when disasters occur.

However, it appears that the human brain is failing us because of the reoccurrence of such tragedies and how we respond to them. So, I often ask myself the following rhetorical questions: *Has the human brain failed humanity? Are leaders of countries in areas prone to natural disasters investing enough in weather research? Do governments earmark enough funds in their yearly budgets for handling emergencies? Can it be possible that everyone believes such natural disasters will occur only on a future date? Is science helping us?*

Many other issues still eat at my soul, but I am unsure if I can think up solutions. I am also not sure if science has the way forward for us. For example, I wonder why women are paid less money than their male counterparts in some places while they are doing the same job. I also wonder why people seek external factors in the hope of obtaining internal validation. When I say people, I mean straight men and women, lesbians, gays, bisexuals, transgender people, and those who are questioning who they are.

CHAPTER 11
Effective Teaching and Engaged Learning

Competent teachers steer their minds to impart knowledge similarly as engaged students drive their minds to acquire knowledge.

*H*aving been involved in educational practices across continents for more than two decades, I am aware of many components of education, including teaching and learning. While both aspects are integral parts of schooling, they have areas of divergence. In the absence of computers and artificial intelligence, teaching implies the existence of a living, breathing human being who receives tutelage. Often, we refer to such a human being as an apprentice, a disciple, learner, pupil, scholar, student, or by other names. Teaching does not happen in a vacuum, and no one can claim to be an educator or an imparter of knowledge in the absence of someone to be taught.

In contrast, learning can take place without the

existence of a living, breathing human being who teaches. Some of the labels we give those who teach include adviser, assistant, coach, disciplinarian, educator, faculty member, guide, instructor, instructional leader, lecturer, mentor, preceptor, professor, pundit, teacher, and trainer, to name a few. In almost 30 years of teaching, I have understood that human beings can learn or record a positive change in their behavior without encountering someone with titles such as those listed above. In spite of our technological advancements, learning can take place without the aid of computers and artificial intelligence, unlike the case with teaching.

Undoubtedly, a well-crafted, systematic curriculum or course of instruction delivered by effective teachers to ready learners tends to be effective, highly productive, and capable of leading to a quick attainment of instructional objectives. However, I have been involved for long enough in the teacher-learner dynamics that I can confidently say that teaching is the most misunderstood profession in the world. Human society puts an undue burden on teachers in the hope that teachers are the ones who will solve societal problems. Such an unrealistic expectation has, in turn, bred a crop of overstressed teachers who vent their frustration on innocent and unsuspecting learners.

To ease the burden on teachers, everyone should work towards understanding the dual nature of human beings. Human beings comprise of body and brain, or mind. We often overlook such duality because religious people have included other aspects, such as what they call the soul. I do not dispute the existence of a soul or other human components, but I often limit my discussion about human elements with my students, to body and brain because we can control those two aspects. With such control comes the possibility of attaining better outcomes in life, but we should first understand how to steer our brain in the right direction. In other words, there is an attribute every effective teacher and engaged learner possess, which can benefit humanity — the ability to steer their hearts or minds.

If you have learned anything in life, it means that you have experienced mind-steering strategies. Indeed, you know what it means to steer your mind. You will use the same method to drive your brain towards achieving better outcomes in other areas of your life. Before I elaborate on those strategies, let us take a closer look at the human body and mind. The well-being of human beings depends on the amicable and equitable functioning of the mind and body. Both human aspects require proper nurturing. The body needs healthy food, drink, adequate shelter in a clean environment, and physical stimulation. The mind requires a systematic and constructive course of instruction. In actions involving the body and mind, remember that the mind controls and dominates the body. Ironically, the mind functions with whatever fuel it has been given.

The mind manages our perceptions, sensory and

motor activities, including the way we think. It is common knowledge that the human mind has a conscious and an unconscious component. Our conscious mind comprises of objective and subjective phases. In short, the mind has many parts that are not within the scope of this book to explain, but for our purposes, we will limit our usage of the mind and its terminology to the conscious, objective, subconscious, and subjective. Effective teaching targets the human brain. It is similar to what people call indoctrination. The moment a teacher gets the minds of his or her learners to align with the instructional objectives, the rest becomes history. Such mind-centered teaching explains why some people will quickly drink poison, following the direction of their instructional leader, when they know that their actions will end their lives.

Such teaching also explains why some people agree to strap explosives around their bodies to detonate in the midst of innocent people. The people who drank poison and those who strapped bombs on their bodies are engaged learners, while those who directed them to do so are effective teachers. Economic status or level of educational attainment makes no difference, which explains why we have seen economically well to do students and professionals who have advanced degrees in fields such as law, engage in suicide bombing. Nevertheless, such activity represents a misdirection of energy. Human beings use three main mediums for acquiring knowledge: the objective, subjective, and subconscious medium. A brief common sense breakdown of these media will suffice. For the objective medium, it consists of the faculties of seeing, hearing, feeling, tasting, and smelling. Out of these five senses, humans frequently use the faculties of sight, hearing, and touch in the acquisition of knowledge.

Unfortunately, these three and the other two often suffer from functional, physical, spatial, and temporal limitations. As a result, diseases and physical deformities can cause them to be defective. For example, blindness or vision impairment and deafness are instances of functional limitations. In terms of distance about a particular object, we know that distance varies according to the faculty in use. None of the five senses can be of any use unaided. The whole human body has to be physically present before we can feel, hear, see, smell, or taste. In other words, we cannot see things that are not visible to our naked eyes or listen to sounds that occurred before we came in hearing distance. Our ability to feel, smell, and taste depend on our proximity to the objects that arouse their sensation. No wonder humanity has produced various gadgets to aid the sense faculties to overcome their limitations.

Some of such instruments are earphones, scanning machines, microphones, spectacles, telephones, wireless transmission equipments, radars, radios, and smell sensors. While scientists are at work daily to improve these gadgets, they have to endure their functional limitations and the challenges of our convoluted physical conditions. As such, humans are uncertain if what they claim to see, hear, feel, taste or smell are the solid, liquid or gaseous matters that are realities to us. Such uncertainty explains why we should know about atoms and vibrations, as well as their functions. The sensation of perception we experience with the senses listed above is the result of an impression on specific nerve centers in our body of the vibratory impulses or waves generated by the discreet, continuous motion of the atoms of the perceived objects.

Approximately, all objects or matter are the same. Every one of them is composed of atoms and molecules. What differentiates one physical object from another is the rate at which it vibrates. On the other hand, the frequency of vibrations depends on the number of electrons, protons, and neutrons in the atoms of each of the physical objects. Other vibratory impulses, which we may or may not be conscious of, can also interfere with the desires that arouse our senses of perception. Thus, the object of perception has to be present before the objective mind can function. It is not the case with the subjective mind. So, when we talk of steering our mind towards our desires, it is analogous to taking a journey with our subjective mind to any location of our choice.

Humans think and reason with their subjective minds. The most critical aspect of thinking and reasoning is that what we think and reason about does not have to be present. Our subjective mind functions mostly over abstract phenomenons such as affection, aspiration, cognition, conation, conception, deductive and inductive reasoning, imagination, observation, and volition, among others. While performing these, the subjective mind is open to internal and external stimuli and influences. The perceptions and views we condone through our five senses generate the external stimuli. Such stimuli are mitigated or aggravated by factors like the nature and character of the perceived objects, where we are in life, our associations, occupation, personal interests, popular culture, level of education, and our health status. For the internal influences, they often emanate from our affections and sentiments, acquired dispositions, subconscious promptings, and instinctive urges, to name a few.

The Subconscious: Steering Your Mind

Unlike what classical psychologists want us to believe, the subconscious mind is in a class of its own. It is a network of autonomous nerves that control and direct the automatic functions of the body, such as our heartbeats. Such control is independent of the cerebrospinal system of nerves of whose activities we have awareness. Nevertheless, both are linked together. The subconscious mind reasons deductively. As a result, our subconscious mind accepts information which reaches it from the objective and subjective sections of our conscious mind. It processes what has been received and executes the conclusions that are infallibly deducible from the information it received. For example, if the objective and subjective components of your conscious mind tell your subconscious mind that Japan is in North America, that is what you will answer in an examination if anyone asks such a question, regardless of the circumstance.

That is why some people still believe, in this day and age, that other human beings are inferior, especially those that are not of the same racial group as them. These people may have grown up in homes where this perspective held sway. The subconscious mind never errs in the performance of allotted functions. If the conclusions which it manifests are wrong, it is because of the inaccurate information supplied to it from the beginning. The influence of your subconscious mind is what gives you the confidence to tell people that you will see them the next day at a specific time, even though you can't control events from that moment to the promised time. If you are willing to feed your subconscious mind and follow it up with appropriate action, your subconscious mind will use its limitless powers to steer other parts of your body to accomplish what you want. A vast number of school teachers are unaware that this is what they do daily. As educators plan their lessons and draw their instructional objectives, they feed their subconscious mind. When they teach and model what they are teaching, they add the action component.

Similarly, engaged learners are those students who have understood the conscious and unconscious mind dynamics. So, is your life going in the direction you desire? Is your mind steered towards better outcomes? If you answered in the negative, you now know what to do. Change what you are feeding your subconscious mind, take action toward where you want to be, and you will get a different result. In all history, effective teachers and engaged learners have followed this simple process. Perhaps, that explains why many people expect teachers to solve more societal problems. Unfortunately, no one can embark on the above process on behalf of another person. It is a personal thing, a quest you have to fulfill for yourself.

CHAPTER 12

Belief Literacy Steps

What would you call someone who knows what to do to become a better person but refuses to do that?

I have seen many of my students give multiple interpretations to the same situation. Such an instructional outcome aligns with my teaching philosophy, which I communicate to my students at the beginning of every semester. I encourage them to form the habit of questioning everything we discuss in class, including my conclusions. At any opportunity I get, I tell them to refrain from accepting everything I say hook, line, and sinker. As such, they consider me an unconventional professor, but I am not. One day in class, a sophomore commented that I was attempting to stop them from doing what they have done their entire academic life.

"Ihuoma, can you please, tell me what you mean by that?" I asked. She hesitated, but I encouraged her to go ahead and explain what she meant by that.

"My friends and I have always looked up to our teachers as excellent sources of knowledge and people whose conclusions are often satisfactory," she said. The entire class appeared surprised when I told her that I was like her.

"So, what changed you?" she asked.

"I changed during my doctoral studies at a place where almost everyone in my department believed that we formed knowledge as we progressed," I replied.

"And so?" another asked.

"Your teachers may not be able to keep up with the changing nature of knowledge. So, my doctoral teachers and I believe that learners should build on their experiences and figure out meanings as they progress in the learning process. To do that, they should filter new information through what they already know," I explained. "Because our backgrounds vary," I continued, "we are bound to see things differently."

I also gave them a caveat: "What I said is just one of many ways to explain teaching and learning, I may be wrong."

"What, then, is your point?" another asked.

"None of you should consider what I have described as being the right way because it could be erroneous," I concluded. Some of my students said I was confusing them. Some said they agreed with me, and some wondered aloud the importance of understanding the dynamics of teaching and learning. I ended the class by telling them that they had arrived at the exact location I wanted them to be, a place where they should decide for themselves.

Similar to my students, we interpret things based on our conscious and unconscious worldviews. I should also add that many factors determine these worldviews. Our attitudes, beliefs, desires, emotions, experiences, and ideas are some of the factors that actuate how we view and interpret things in life. Additionally, our subconscious can also be influenced by the same factors indicated above. Factors like social media information affect our attitudes, beliefs, desires, ideas, decisions, and choices we make. I have also understood that the human brain is the center-piece of the elements which contribute to how we perceive and explain issues. I like to tell my students stories about how each component of a human body is essential. I often end each tale by pointing out my respect and admiration for the human brain, which I use synonymously with the human mind because it is exceptional. Early in life, I understood that success and failure were dependent on what happened in our brain. To succeed in life, I believe that we should explore the enormous power of our mind.

The English language is not enough to describe the capability of the human brain. What gives me comfort, however, is that scientists have completed numerous studies about the brain and its many components, including how these components work with our nervous system. Further excellent research has also been conducted to demonstrate the power of the brain when you make or state intent, however whimsical. Nevertheless, it is not my intent to engage in any form of academic discourse about the human brain in this book, but I will encourage you to imagine a simple scenario to help you to form an opinion about the human mind and the power of a simple intent.

Imagine you are walking down the middle of a busy road on a Monday morning, and vehicles are charging toward you. If you are sane, sober, and not suicidal, you will quickly turn away when you see a vehicle about to hit you head-on. In an instant, your eyes would alert your brain through direct sensory information, which would automatically trigger your legs to move your whole body out of the road to avoid being run over. Your mind acts this way because of your knowledge of oncoming vehicles, which trample pedestrians. Such knowledge is derived from personal experience or the experiences of others, which influences your thoughts and forms your beliefs. I use the word *experience* as a reference to emotion, something you have heard or read, a sight, smell, or taste. So, as you see the oncoming vehicle, you think that you will die if it runs you over.

Because you don't want to kill yourself (as it is not your intent), your brain suggests to other parts of your body to quickly exit the road. It could also go the other way. If you have experienced a head-on collision with a car on multiple occasions in the past and did not perish, your brain will suggest to other parts of your body that you won't die if you are hit by a car that Monday morning. Consequently, your brain will encourage other parts of your body to support your legs as you continue to walk down the middle of that busy road, in spite of multiple vehicles coming toward you. It could also be the case that you have not had any experience with collisions, but other people have shared their experiences with you, and you have accepted them to be true. Such acceptance built your belief system and influenced your reaction to a vehicle approaching you while strolling down a busy road.

Hopefully, this simple scenario shone a light on how the human brain functions. Although we believe many things without knowing that we do so, our brain is the center of such beliefs. Once we believe, our brain triggers other parts of our body to accomplish what we believe. If our belief involves things that are entirely out of our control, our brain soothes our nerves and suggests to our entire body that what we believe will happen. Such brainpower explains why we say things like, *"My flight leaves in 45 minutes," "See you tomorrow, buddy," "Let's catch up over a meal in two days,"* and *"I will be there next month for the event,"* without any guarantee that what we are saying will happen.

Flights can take off and crash within five minutes. Most of those people who told their friends they would see them the following day are now unable to say where their friends are because those friends died before the anticipated date.

It is common to plan to meet someone in two days, and it ends up becoming the longest two days ever because one person never showed up. We have made promises to be somewhere the following month but failed to fulfill them. Human beings understand their inability to predict what will happen in the next minute, yet they make commitments with one another about future events. As I said in the prologue, many factors contribute to such behavior.

Nonetheless, I have observed through many years of interacting with people that we enter into such obligations because of our beliefs. Although we are not always aware, we often think that we will be alive and in good health to fulfill our commitments. Interestingly, our ape-like predecessors were not like this because they had a fixed behavioral pattern.

Only humans are capable of reasoning in a direction that suggests the possibility of accomplishing something at a future date without evidence. We follow such a line of thinking because of the way nature wired our brain. We tend to tilt toward our dominant thoughts. As such, when we are in a state of sanity we can produce and believe sensations, images, or ideas in our mind and, eventually, experience them precisely as we thought. We also have willpower, which means that we have control over our impulses. Willpower is like freedom; it implies that we can choose to do something or decide not to. So, if we can set an intent, visualize the outcome or something close, believe that it can happen, and it happens because of our brainpower and belief, it follows that we can attain favorable outcomes in life if we extend such capability to other areas. To achieve such a feat, however, I am suggesting you embrace a three-step process, which I termed *Belief Literacy Steps (BLS)*. Below are the steps:

STEP 1
Identify Your Thoughts

Have you ever found yourself at an unfamiliar place instead of your desired destination because you took a wrong turn or exit? If yes, you have experienced what it means to get lost en route to your destination. If you called someone for help, the first question most likely to have been asked would be *"Where are you?."* Your answer to that question would help the person determine how to give you directions. Perhaps, such a query explains why teachers begin to teach from known to the unknown. Or why they provide course outlines or syllabi as a guide to help learners comfortably navigate the unknown. Effective teachers often design instruction to match the learners' level and gradually move up as if they are climbing a ladder to take learners to the desired skill level. Like such teachers, it is essential for those who want to take *Belief Literacy Steps* to begin by pointing out where they are in life, and to read their thoughts to identify and understand the ideas they hold toward the circumstances they want to alter. A belief literate thought reader should answer questions such as, *"What is this?" "Where am I on this?" "What do I know about this?" "What do I want this to be?"* and *"How do I get this to meet my expectation?"*

Where you are in life may be assessed using factors such as your thoughts and beliefs about resources and how to acquire them. Other life factors include our ideas and opinions about personal identity, vocation, occupation, recreation, God, education, health, food, community, justice, and relationships, to mention a few. Once you identify the factors, what you understand about the scenario, and your beliefs about them, you are ready to take the remaining steps. In other words, it is time to take the next step when you have identified where you are and what you know about your current situation or circumstance.

Have you ever seen law enforcement officers in real life responding to an active shooter incident? Did you notice that they allow anyone with raised hands to leave the crime scene? Should the shooter drop his or her ammunition and join the crowd with uplifted hands, the same law enforcement officials searching for the shooter will escort him or her away from the crime scene. Even if the perpetrator's description matches what the law enforcement officers have, they will not swoop on the shooter because their initial priority is to read and to understand the crime scene.

So, the first step of *BLS* centers on learning the situation. Scan the case and take in as much information from your current circumstances and surroundings as fast as you can. Do not analyze. It is only time for a quick assessment. As such, you should learn to recognize the circumstance and your thoughts on the position of things. With proper practice, one could complete the above step in a matter of seconds.

STEP 2

Evaluate Your Thoughts

One should assess the outcome of the first *Belief Literacy Step* quickly. The purpose of the second Belief Literacy Step is to make sure you have identified what you know about where you stand and the circumstances surrounding you. Could you say that you know where you are? Could you also affirm that you can identify or list what you know about where you are in numerical order? Perhaps, you answered *yes* to the questions above. Then, you are ready to answer the final queries of this step: *"Where do I need to be?" What will get me there?"* and *"How will I know I am there?"* Your answers to these last set of questions are what will build and become the core of your belief. Once you *believe*, you are ready to take the final *Belief Literacy step.* Follow your instincts, set your intent, and do not worry about being right or wrong because the steps are cyclic.

As such, you can come back and repeat them until you attain your desired objectives. Also, you do not need to have identified all that is necessary before moving on to the final step. Most people get stuck, and analysis paralysis sets in because they become preoccupied with perfection. However, it helps to weigh your answers to the questions about where you need to be, what will lead you there, and how you will know you are at your destination, in the light of reasoning and good conscience. Indeed, the second step requires you to assess your perceptions and perspectives, determine where you want to go, what action will get you there, and what it will be like when you get there. It calls for designing appropriate steps or setting a clear intent to take you to your desired destination. The answers you get here will become your *beliefs*. As with the previous step, it does not require much time. One can also accomplish this phase within seconds.

STEP 3
Take Action

Finally, step three is to implement the actions you have designed. Just make a move! The world is in constant motion. As such, we have to take action so we can be in sync with the time. Do something. Do not fold your arms.

What did you say would take you to your desired destination? What are the simple steps? If viewing the measures as strategies will help, then do so. Implement them without hesitation. As with previous stages, you should also be swift in this step. It is helpful to understand that it is okay to fail and that there is no need to worry about being right or wrong. Just take action and be ready to start over if you do not achieve your desired results.

Example of BLS: Someone offers a 15-year-old boy or girl an alcoholic drink at a social gathering. No one is asking for identification documents, but within seconds the boy or girl decides to take the *BLS* and use brainpower to think about the offer. Something similar to the following might go through his or her mind: *"This person just offered me an alcoholic drink. I know I can become an alcoholic later in life if I start drinking at my age. I know that the consumption of alcoholic beverages could lead me to perform poorly in my school work. Also, alcohol might mess up my kidneys, which could lead to my death. I need to finish school and move on to college. I also need to grow up to be a decent adult citizen, not become an alcoholic. Accepting this offer and consuming alcohol will not get me to college or help me grow up to become a respectable adult. As such, I should say no and walk away."*

Such internal dialogue will take a couple of seconds. So, as the person is offering the alcoholic drink, the 15-year-old is saying no and stepping away.

To begin the process described above, we should first

structure our thinking. Many things around us are pushing us toward unnecessary and distracting thoughts. While it is helpful, sometimes, to entertain negative thoughts, especially when we want to execute negative actions (Don't we? We do that from time to time. Like when we want to be mean to others), you should bear in mind that you are the one to bear the consequences. Random and unproductive thoughts cause us to lead barren lives. After thinking, we should make decisions and follow them up with actions. Decide on the course you want your life to take and then make a move, because there is a vast difference between thinking and taking action. You are responsible for yourself. Take control. Create what you want from your life.

Finally, it is essential to point out that humans have conscious and unconscious thoughts, as well as a very active and fluid subconscious, as noted in one of the preceding chapters. What we deliberately profess, or choose to believe, in guiding our lives are our conscious thoughts. Our unconscious thoughts are automatic because they emanate from our core beliefs, and sometimes, we are unable to choose them. Some unconscious thoughts come to our minds even before we have time to think because they represent our true selves. An example of conscious and unconscious thoughts will suffice here.

We know that most people in the United States mix with people from many different racial backgrounds in school, at work, and during sporting events, to name a few places. They smile, laugh, and play with one another, but as soon as they return home, they reenter their little race-colored cocoons. If such people needed to talk about their fellow students, coworkers, or people they met at sporting events to family members in the comfort of their homes, most of them would use racial descriptors in disrespectful manners, contrary to how they had behaved while mingling with said people. Such coworkers use their conscious thoughts while interacting at their place of work, learning environment, or sports arenas, but employ their unconscious thoughts at home.

Such unconscious thoughts may have been planted into the subconscious through years of unconscious absorption of environmental and mass media stimuli. Eventually, they surface as conscious thoughts and actions later in life. *Belief Literacy Steps* will only work for those who use their unconscious thoughts. The good news, however, is that human beings can control their thinking process, both at the conscious and the unconscious level. You now know what to do to steer your mind towards becoming a better person. What should we call you if you refuse to comply?

section two

CHAPTER 13
Botswana the Beautiful

Bots. is a quintessential country of opposites in Africa.

As the airplane descended, I peeped through the window. It appeared we were going to land on grassland. "Where am I going? What is happening to me?" I railed at myself. Shortly, the airplane commenced its final descent. What appeared to be a large area of grassland from the air turned out to be Gaborone city, a place bustling with friendly people who were always smiling. Gabs or GC is the capital of Botswana. The airport shares the same name as the first president of the country, Sir Seretse Khama. So, it is unlikely you will forget the airport anytime soon, since the name is well known. In short, the name is synonymous with the history of Botswana. My arrival at the airport was the culmination of a journey from Houston in Texas, where everything is big. I had lived in Texas for many years and recently completed a doctorate in literacy from a college in the Texas state university system. A public university in Botswana hired me to teach academic literacy courses.

Literacy is a broad area of study, but academic literacy courses are those courses you take in college to help you navigate academic life successfully. Academic literacy courses include courses in research, which teach students how to collect and examine particulars to help them explain things. It also involves classes that expose students to numeracy, reading, writing, and how to think like scholars. Because college is an academic community, attendees are expected to think and behave in a certain manner. Such an expectation explains why institutions of higher learning require that students take academic literacy courses. Some institutions prefer to have experts teach academic literacy courses instead of any available professor. Most universities attach importance to academic literacy courses, which explains why some of them go the extra mile to import academic literacy professors from overseas, as was my case. In a nutshell, academic literacy courses expose students to ways of thinking, behaving, and living in a world of scholarship. Academic literacy courses are also life skill courses that prepare students and non-students for life in school and society.

Bayana stood at the arrival lounge with a placard that had my name. Like everyone else, she was smiling. I reached where she stood, and the following ensued.

"Hi, that is my name," I said, pointing at the placard.

Almost instantaneously, she said, "Dumelang rra."

I stared at her in confusion. She quickly reverted to the English language to introduce herself and signaled the way to a car waiting in the airport's parking lot. *Dumelang* is how Batswana say hello, and rra is how to say, sir. Never forget those two words because you will hear them every day of your life in Botswana. If you are a woman, *rra* will change to *nma*. The driver introduced himself as Mojeed. He smiled and spoke gently. Bayana and Mojeed began to discuss in Setswana and English language once I entered the car. The steering wheel of their vehicle was on a different side from where it would be in Nigeria or the United States. We were also driving on a different side of the road that reminded me of the United Kingdom. Periodically, Bayana interjected and told me our location. She also told me how many more kilometers we needed to cover before reaching the college town.

I attempted to quickly convert kilometers into miles in my head. Before I could finish my conversion, I froze because everything looked different. I saw large numbers of cattle grazing by the side of the road. I also noticed that barbwire fences were preventing the cattle from entering the highway. Bayana and Mojeed conversed intensely. I wanted to analyze their speech because they were code-switching, but that was my first time hearing the language called Setswana. So, my brain became fuzzy. Code-switching is what happens when speakers switch from one language to another in the course of conversation.

"How can you analyze what you do not know?" I asked myself. I continued to observe their facial expressions. I attempted reading their lips and gestures to understand what they were saying. I knew I could grasp what they were saying almost instantaneously. I have read throughout my career. I reminded myself that my area of doctoral study was reading. So, I could read anything in the world, including human beings. However, I was in a problematic situation, for I was unable to read or comprehend their speech.

Fortunately, I knew why I could not read them. I needed to understand the language before I could read the speakers' lips. So, I sat back and resigned to my fate at the back of the car. Helplessly, I battled with myself over my choice to work in such a strange place. Approximately two and a half hours later, we arrived at the college town. Bayana and Mojeed helped me check into a hotel. As the duo had completed their mission, they departed. From the next day forward, different drivers transported me to and from the university. About two weeks into my stay, I moved into the faculty housing unit of my host university. I also purchased a car to navigate Bots, as we fondly called the country. My residence was in a suburb known as Serowe, about 45 minutes from the college. I would later move to Phakalana, a posh suburb that is a few kilometers from Gaborone. Serowe reminded me of other parts of the country I had visited. Living in Botswana was like studying words and opposites. I saw a vast landmass with few human inhabitants. Affluence and abject poverty stared at me at the same time. Often, I noticed beautiful mansions sharing neighborhoods with ugly buildings.

Flashy cars shared the road with rickety-looking, locally made donkey carts. I saw world-class roadways. Such roadways took me to major cities like Francistown and Maun. However, if I stopped halfway to go to communities that were in between major cities, I would be at the mercy of sandy track roads and paths that looked like they could lead only to farmlands. However, I held my breath and did not write those roads off just then. Indeed, those sandy track roads led me to farmlands. They also directed me to houses that shared spaces with farmlands in remote areas. In such farms, I saw people cultivating agricultural products. As I say farms, do not compare them with the average farm in your backyard. I saw people who owned farms of industrial magnitude. At other times such roads took me to farms where people were rearing cattle. I saw signs that referred to such places as cattle farms, but the people I met there called such sites cattle posts. I saw many teens going to school, and I saw other teens chilling at home. Those teens who were at home told me that their families could not afford to pay school fees.

Unbeknownst to them, I knew they were lying because the government pays tuition for them. Their country is among the few countries in Africa where the government pays school fees for folks to attend school. That was not all that I witnessed. The government also pays citizens who double as college students. My students called it their monthly allowance, but I called it paying someone to go to school. In spite of such governmental generosity, many did not attend school. I saw a bubbling nightlife where people, including me, drank alcohol like water. I saw signs that admonished us not to drink and drive. I also saw people drinking and driving, literally. I witnessed the government increase taxation of alcoholic beverages, probably to discourage excessive consumption. Amid the paradox, folks smiled all the time. The country's economy boomed with a high standard of living at an affordable cost for an expatriate.

Most importantly, local foods were irresistible. The presence of nutritious local food could make anyone remain in the country indefinitely. My favorite was Seswaa, made of beef that is mashed into bits and pieces, what we might refer to as pulled beef. The meat was excellent and tasty. I saw cattle grazing in the fields. I witnessed the slaughtering process, following strict standards set by the government. The government regulated everything relating to the cattle business. They even made public announcements urging people to cook meat properly before eating as a way of suppressing contamination. Living in Botswana was like going back to school. I learned many new things about animals, diamonds, mining, and life in general. I consider the country a huge tourist destination where one could visit over and over. Indeed, Bots could be one of, if not the best, place to live in Africa due to the functional state apparatus, including a robust economy. Three weeks flew by quicker than I anticipated. I was hard at work designing a new research course for my students per directives from the dean of the college of sciences and the head of my department. I was also busy developing instruments for assessments while waiting for students to return from the summer holidays. Students returned a few days later, and regular classes began.

My students were the cream of the crop of college students in Botswana. From the way they behaved in class, you could tell they came from the best homes in the country. The curiosity my students exhibited in class was unending and their thirst for knowledge remained unquenched. My students were passionate about scholarship and dedicated to their academics. These students made teaching college fun for me even though some of them mocked me for mispronouncing Setswana words in class. I, too, laughed at some of them who used a British accent to speak Setswana in class. Many years after graduation, some of my students and I keep in touch. As is the case with the job of a college professor, my life in Botswana was centered on community service, research, and teaching. My greatest pleasure in Bots came from speaking to elementary school kids and working with their teachers to design tools for measuring improvement in literacy learning. I also attended lots of conferences.

For one conference, I was in a college in Namibia conferring with colleagues about indigenous knowledge systems in Africa. During a breakaway session, I joined a group discussion on spirituality and witchcraft in African indigenous knowledge. My earlier presentation contained a rhetorical question from one of my research participants: *"Is witchcraft included? University students' perspectives on African indigenous knowledge."* The exchange of ideas during this session prompted me to decide to expand my study. So, I returned to Botswana with the sole aim of broadening my research focus to new horizons. I resolved to explore spirituality and witchcraft in African indigenous knowledge. I also decided to search for strategies to integrate such knowledge into teaching and learning. I would incorporate my cook and gardener into the study. Upon returning to Serowe, my gardener was not at home. He was not present every weekend. So, I had a discussion with my cook about how to reach witchcraft people around town. My cook was also my Setswana language teacher. He was a senior, sixty years of age, with the curiosity and vivacity of a young adult male. He did not consume alcoholic beverages but never forgot to stock up our house bar with drinks from the Kalahari breweries.

As for red and white wine, he insisted they be those imported from neighboring South Africa. We usually had enough drinks to last us for two weekends in a row, even if we had visitors. My man, as we fondly called each other, was endowed with natural wisdom. He proved to be good company because he had a plentitude of sound judgment. My man understood me so well that he knew when I needed to be left alone, and also when I needed companionship. He was a near-expert when it comes to the knowledge of human behavior. I wondered if indeed he had only a sixth-grade education, as he told me. By previously examining my appearance at home, he could describe how my day went at school. He knew exactly what to prescribe in every situation. My man worked like a psychologist who evaluated me and knew the appropriate intervention.

CHAPTER 14

When Research Yields More

Sometimes in life, we search for this but end up finding this, and that.

My man and I often encountered lots of conceptual misunderstandings in our research project. He considered a traditional medical practitioner as being in the same occupation with a witchcraft person, but I disagreed.

An Afro trado-medicine man or woman is a medical practitioner. He or she uses herbs and roots to treat ailments. As such, they are often called herbalists. Witchcraft, on the other hand, involves some form of magic, spells, and meddling with witches and wizards. So, it was tough for my man to assemble appropriate participants for our study. I needed locals who were also witchcraft practitioners and knowledgeable about spirituality in the African context. Our research was grounded in ethnography and involved the use of multiple methods. We planned to identify and do an in-depth study of cases, proposed to observe various situations from different angles, and to conduct a series of interviews with participants. Also, we designed some questionnaires to survey witchcraft practitioners who were not within our reach in Serowe. We hoped that the perspectives of our case participants and the feedback from our survey respondents would enrich our research.

I was excited about our study, but my man was more in charge of sourcing for our participants than I was. Because he was the only one out of the two of us who knew the people and understood the local language, I was at the mercy of his choices. However, I was not concerned because I trusted my man. I taught him how to conduct research almost every evening while relaxing in our garden behind our house. I taught him how to ask questions during academic investigations. I showed him how to prevent his personal views from interfering with his study. I asked him open-ended questions so he could mirror me in the field when we would be out for data collection. I explained to him the differences between journalistic questions and the questions of a researcher. I showed him how research could shape our world into a better place.

My man was a good student. As such, I believed that he was on the same page as I was. My only concern was the language barrier between us. He had an expert knowledge of the Setswana language. He wrote and spoke Setswana fluently, but he had a basic understanding of the English language. His reserve of English words was mainly from the songs of famous western musicians of the mid-1900s. So, he had lots of advantages over me. I did not understand Setswana language beyond what I called survival prompts. Such prompts consisted of courtesy words for greeting people and informing them that I was a new college professor in town. My man and I used gestures to supplement our communication at home as he continued to teach me the Setswana language. Like a captain, he was navigating our research team.

Slightly before 7 pm on a Thursday, we were at a miniature, circular-shaped mud house observing what he called a witchcraft practice session. We accessed the place by making a right turn on an untarred road adjacent to the general hospital while coming from the new mall. There was no way he could translate everything to me at the same time we were observing the ceremony. So, I waited till we got into my car and headed home. The man in charge was a fair-skinned, elderly man with the best smile I had ever seen. He was also exceedingly friendly. He wore a big gown-like robe. I could tell that the color of the gown was white as I gazed at him. My man considered him to be a witch doctor. About 15 people whose ages ranged from 18 to 70 sat in a circular form with the priest in the middle.

We were busy singing and clapping. I did not understand the songs, yet I felt a genuine connection with the group. I heard them say *Badimo*, which I always confused with *Modimo*. One of the two words refers to God, while the other is for ancestors. We took turns answering the witch doctor's questions. The witch doctor progressed according to our seating position. When it came to your turn, you would express your problems and hand over your ritual items. I sent money for my ritual items through my cook earlier. Upon arrival, one of the attendants handed me a bowl containing flour, candles, matches, and some other things I could not identify. According to my man, those attendants were apprentices learning how to become witch doctors. Although it was not required, some people added about five or ten Pula as they presented their bowls to the witch doctor. Pula is the name of the local currency. Five or ten Pula is the equivalent of about two or four US quarters.

The witch doctor would pour out the items in the bowl, light one of the candles, and then ask the owner to state his or her problems. During my turn, the entire group became quiet. My man was interpreting. The witch doctor interjected with some English language making it easier for me to understand my man's explanations. His questions and comments included the following: *"What is the name of your father?"* *"What is the name of your mother?"* *"What are the names of your grandparents?"* *"What are the names of your favorite uncles?"* *"What are the names of your favorite aunts?"* *"What is the name of your village?"* *"No, what* is Houston?" "*Your friend said you are a citizen of Nigeria and America, but what I want to know is neither Houston nor America*" "*What is the name of your village in Nigeria?*" I answered all of his questions. Then he asked the main question: "*What is your problem?*"

"*Nothing, I only want to be part of this group to enable me to understand spirituality in this part of Africa for my research,*" I replied.

I thanked him and expressed my happiness for their kindness in allowing a stranger like me to crash their ceremony.

"You are not a stranger," replied the witch doctor. "The spirits in our congregation recognized your spirits," he concluded. Next, everyone followed the witch doctor outside in a single line. We stood around a fire. An attendant poured all the items from everyone's ritual bowl into the fire as we danced around the fire. An intense prayer ensued. The witch doctor moved from person to person, praying for everyone individually. Each of us knelt near the fire while facing the witch doctor for prayers. The service ended at 2 a.m. on Friday, and we returned home safely. My man prepared some beef sauce due to my unhealthy habit of eating at odd times. It took him forever to cook the beef because he cooked the meat until it became very mushy. We used this sauce to eat sorghum, so I stayed back in the kitchen gisting with my man.

I was also sipping a liquor made with Amarula fruits.

We conversed as the cooking progressed.

"I do not believe that man is doing witchcraft," I said to my cook. "Why was he calling God?" I continued. "Why did he ask me for the names of everyone in my family?" I concluded.

"My man!" he responded, "You call our research witchcraft, that is why I call the man witch doctor."

"He asked for those names because he used their names to pray for you. He called upon the spirit of God and the spirit of your ancestors to protect you. If God and your dead relatives can help you, who among them will help you quicker?" he concluded.

I paused, perplexed. Then I replied, "You are confusing me with this question. How can my dead relatives help me? I believe they are dead and gone."

Smiling, he shocked me with a strange response. "You have too much book in your head, my man. If you did not notice, there were times everyone laughed, but I did not interpret it to you. The witch doctor praised you for having the courage to participate in the ceremony from beginning to end. He said you are also a witch doctor."

As he finished speaking, I noticed the food was ready. It is our rule that no one should dish food for anyone in our house, so my man took some food on his plate. I reached for a plate to dish out some for myself. We relaxed and ate silently at the dining table. After awhile, I broke the silence and said to my man, "You know I am a college professor, not a witch doctor. What we were doing at that place is called participant observation in research. We had to do what they were doing to enable us to understand their mindset."

"You have told me this many times, my man, but why did the witch doctor call you a witch doctor?" he retorted. "Are you a witch doctor in America?"

"No, my man, I am not a witch doctor anywhere in the world, and I am not planning on becoming a witch doctor. My man, you know what I am doing in Botswana, so I will not blame that man if he calls me a witch doctor. As for you, I will not be happy if you join anyone to call me a witch doctor because you know that I am not a witch doctor. Do you think your government will employ me from America to come and do witchcraft in Botswana?" I queried. "Please, let us not derail our research."

After a second visit to the witch doctor's place with my man, I started to go alone. I went for about ten weeks without him. There was no more need for an interpreter. All the people who attended the sessions were friendly. By my fourth visit, they had accepted me as the American who did not speak or understand Setswana. So, when they needed to talk to me, they asked for volunteers who could speak some English. As for me, I knew the drill. Each time I got there, I would head straight to the fireplace. A big earthen pot with lots of leaves and herbs was always cooking on firewood. There was a big bowl with many cups. I would take a cup, scoop medication from the big earthen pot, settle into a corner, and slowly drink the herbal mixture. After drinking, I would wait for the day's ceremony to begin. There were days they instructed me to take a bath for cleansing.

Bathing at the witch doctor's place was the most adventurous thing I did in Bots. It usually involved standing in a big bathing bowl inside the sanctuary and scooping water from a smaller bucket while ensuring that no water spilled out. The bathing water had lots of medicinal leaves. There were times they gave me herbal drinks that doubled as laxatives. I purged for a couple of days and returned for prayers. Eventually, I interviewed the witch doctor on a Sunday evening, and I confirmed my suspicion that he was not into any form of witchcraft. I told him about my uncle Bryan and our family ceremony. He said both him and my uncle were engaging in ancestral worship. His explanations helped me to understand the belief systems of my formative years. A few days later, I donated a dozen plastic chairs to them so we could have a place to sit instead of sitting on logs and broken chairs. I also encouraged those who came with injuries sustained from farm implements to go to the hospital across the road instead of waiting for prayers. Healthcare is free in Botswana for its citizens, courtesy of the government.

I was in my office at the university the next morning, which was a Monday, when one of my students walked in. My office door was always open; I did not require my students to make an appointment before coming to my office. My policy was that my students were allowed to walk into my office anytime, as long as the door was open. They knew that my office door only closed when I was not on campus. Also, my students were aware that any unexcused absence from my class would result in a reduction of points in their continuous assessment grades. If any of my students missed lectures or tutorials up to three times in a semester, he or she would not score an *A* grade even if he or she scored 100 percent. They knew I would deduct points to bring the student's score down to a *B* grade.

I explained this policy to my students on the first day of every semester of my career as a college professor. Settling into one of the chairs in my office, he began asking me about my weekend. This was not unusual because my students were comfortable chatting with me. They viewed me as more like a pal and mentor than their professor. I reached for the class attendance list kept by my teaching assistant and noticed that the student in front of me had less than perfect attendance. *Perhaps, our conversation will trickle down to his reasons for missing classes,* I told myself. However, our discussion did not take such detour. After exchanging pleasantries and asking about my whereabouts the past weekend, he showed me pictures and videos of what he did over the weekend. He stood in front of what appeared to be a congregation of churchgoers, like someone who was preaching. So, I moved his cell phone closer as I watched with great admiration. I began to think that someone was brainwashing my student. Instead of behaving like a scholar in an academic environment, my student was being influenced negatively. As I gazed at the cell phone, I noticed that my student was the one preaching. He was the one praying for the congregation. He was also the one praying for someone who appeared to have crippled legs, but was trying to walk.

Watching agape, I expressed my surprise to him.

"The man you see in the video was walking because of Jesus," he said. "Jesus makes disabled people walk, and you can see that in the Bible, sir. We need to invite God into our lives by confessing our sins and then pray for the Holy Spirit to teach us before reading the Bible," he added with a smile.

Does Jesus have an orthopedic clinic in Botswana? I wondered in my mind. I remembered my new faculty orientation. I remembered the past ten weeks and how I had been exploring spiritualism and witchcraft in the country. I also remembered lots of information about Botswana, but nothing came to my mind relating to what I watched in the video. *How come my student does not appear scholarly in his thought process?* I wondered. *What kind of foolishness has my student encountered? Did I not teach my students to question everything in life? I know I have taught them to avoid accepting everything without asking questions, as scholars in the making.*

How come my student is very comfortable in his reasoning about Jesus and the Bible? Does my student know that Jesus was only a first-century Jew who lived in Israel? Does he even know Jesus' real name?

I respected my students, so I chose not to vocalize any of the questions plaguing my mind. As a student-centered scholar, I imposed on myself the obligation to help my students. None of my students can recall any negative moment in class, including my written feedback. I was not ready to spoil that record. So, I thanked him for sharing such information with me and told him to keep it up as he neared the door. His face beamed with smiles. What caused my student to exhibit such a high level of passion? Alone, I began to ponder within myself. What does my student know about the Bible? Does he know that most things in the Bible won't make sense to him due to translatory irregularities? Does he even see the relationship between the Bible and the Hebrew language? Is he aware that he may lose up to 50 percent of the meaning of Biblical content if he does not understand the Hebrew language? I pondered these and more questions as I returned to my work.

CHAPTER 15

Finding Purpose in an Unlikely Place

What we look at does not always determine what we see.

I questioned myself endlessly. *Did God direct my student to talk to me? Could God even do such a thing? If God was involved in the meeting I had with my student, why did He allow it to happen? Could God use my student to make a physically challenged man walk? If the answer is yes, how come He has not healed my local friends who are living with HIV/AIDS? By the way, who is God? Where could God be?* I know that God is in me, but why did my student stop by my office for such a conversation? Does my student know about my research? I know I have not discussed my research with members of his class. Why did he come to me at the time he did? Considering our activities the previous weekend, I wondered why my student and I were engaged in spirituality at the same time.

I became engulfed by restlessness. I felt there should have been more to what happened. Could it be that my fans and cheerleaders spoke to me through my student? What my student said to me were things I have heard from other people on several occasions. None of what he said was new to me. Some of my mentees and colleagues in the department are ordained pastors, but I did well in avoiding them because my conversations with them depressed me. Everything about them reminded my other colleagues and I how sinful we were and how we would roast in hell someday. The way they walked and talked in our office depicted righteousness, so almost everyone avoided them. Because most of them were also doctoral candidates, I mentored them more and limited our discussions to scholarship. However, my student was different. He behaved like an everyday person, connected to the realities of life. His visit to my office was also typical. He only shared a video, showed me some pictures, had a quick conversation, and left.

"How come I am still in my office thinking about all that transpired hours after he had gone?" I asked myself.

So, I packed my books and headed to my residence in Serowe. I concluded that I had failed myself and the college. Yes, I did not keep my student busy enough with the scholarly activities I was hired to do. He would not have had time for such things to steal his attention. On second thought, I said to myself that my student only shared his belief system with me, so it should not have been my business to get involved. He has a right to believe in anything and exercise his beliefs anyhow he deems appropriate. As an American, I am aware that the religious view of my student falls within the First Amendment of the US constitution, which protects everyone. I also know that Americans define freedom of religion as the right to practice any religion or not practice a religion. So, I should not have worried about my student as I did. However, as a teacher, I am also aware that the beliefs of a teacher and his or her philosophical perspectives influence instructional behavior. I know that teachers behave like parents, sometimes believing that they know what is best for their students. So, I am guilty in that respect. Nevertheless, my students call me unconventional because I have always acknowledged in class that they know more than I do in certain areas.

Each of the times I shared my shortcomings in the classroom, I ended up relating it to the digital age. My students are more digital-savvy than I am, but I have had to behave like them to drive instruction. For example, in 2016, I chased a particular group of my students to where they congregated online. While in their virtual community, I signed up for a Twitter account to make an announcement even though I believed they should check their college emails and message board. Joining my students on social network sites or communicating with them using digital messaging apps taught me that my students open up more for discussion in technologically driven environments.

So, I concluded that I would use a couple of text messages to invite my student back to the office. A second visit would enable us to discuss the issues he raised during his previous visit, I reasoned. However, I concluded that I should prepare myself before meeting him again. As a teacher, I appreciate the fact that I ought to begin from what my student knows to take him to what he does not. So, I had to read the Bible and acquire some information that would help me convince him to be serious with his studies. Busy students do not have the time to document such information on their cell phones, I assured myself. Unfortunately, the problem in reading the Bible is that I'm not too fond of some of the views expressed in the book. I consider the text an instrument of oppression. In my undergraduate and graduate degree classes in political science, I studied how European colonial powers used the Bible and Christianity to conceal their exploitative tendencies and plundered Africa. Unlike many parts of Asia, like in China and India, the British took advantage of the friendliness of Africans to meddle in their religious beliefs. Shortly after that, they forced Africans to discard their indigenous religious beliefs. I have also seen a version of the Bible that was authorized by King James of England. Was England not part of that island country that once colonized almost the whole world? Why would King James approve of a book that would benefit my student?

I became angry. *How could I have such a boy as my student? Does it mean he has not read any of the history books about Africa?*

Alone, I yelled, "The Bible is an instrument of capitalism! I do not like what the Bible says about the man who has little. He will be a victim of appropriation for the benefit of the man who has more. That is capitalistic. Why did the Bible say that people should not steal? Do some people not sometimes steal out of necessity? Would anyone even take someone else's property if there was no private ownership?"

With these ideas burning in my mind, I felt strong enough to engage with my student. However, I reasoned that it was important to reread the Bible before I arranged the meeting with him. Maybe the Bible had indeed been revised and updated. So, I concluded that I must check again to see if these contradictions were still present within the pages of the Bible.

My cook had gone home to be with his family, so I was alone. He would have appeased my triggered spirit. It was not the weekend that my gardener was scheduled to come, so I was completely by myself. I reached for my Caribbean rum, had a few sips, and stepped into my study. It was exactly midnight. I began combing through my shelves for a Bible. There were three of them in my house. One was a present from my mom when I left home for college. The other was a gift from the World Bible School during the early 1990s. My third bible cost an arm and a leg. It was a big study bible I purchased many years ago for a research project. As a scholar, I enjoy reading the scripture as reference material. I also have the Sutras, Vedas, Quran, and many other religious literatures. I could not recall the exact number of books I owned, so it was likely that one of my Bibles was stuck somewhere in the stack of books on my shelf. After a few seconds of scouring, I located one, and to my chagrin, recalled what my student said about the need to pray before reading the Bible. So, I prayed.

"Dear God, I know you live in my life. A few hours ago, my student said I needed to invite you into my life, so the Holy Spirit will help me to understand the Bible. I am a sinner, kindly forgive me of my sins and come into my life. Please, send the Holy Spirit to show me Bible passages I can use to talk to my student because I believe he should concentrate on his studies and not mix classwork with religious activities."

I flipped to a random verse on a random page that read that the Holy Spirit interprets the Bible. It progressed to say that no man could understand the things of God except by the spirit of God, who gives discernment. Those words sobered me up instantly. Clearly, I did not understand the Bible because I was reading the Bible as if it were an academic document. At that moment, I felt goosebumps emanate all over my body. I turned a couple of pages and saw where it read that the letter could kill, but the spirit gives life, and that was enough to make me question my reasoning.

CHAPTER 16

Humanity Created God and Religion

Perhaps, by worshiping inanimate objects out of fear, men and women created God and religion, for which they deserve some commendation.

*M*aybe, it was only a coincidence that I opened the Bible to pages containing information that sobered me up. So, I avoided sharing the experience with anyone to avoid appearing silly. If I told members of my family, they would ask me to remind them the last time I was treated for malaria. But this had nothing to do with malaria. A single mosquito had not bitten me for 20 years. As is commonly the case with my family members, I was sure they would probe further by raining more questions on me like, *"Is your blood pressure high?" "Have you been consuming lots of alcoholic beverages?" "Are you still living alone?"* Also, I did not want to share my experience with my cook or gardener because they would think I had been drinking without them. My experience of sobriety because of the information from random pages in the Bible was similar to what we talked about for laughs over drinks. As such, anyone who brought up such a topic when we were not drinking was assumed to have been drinking secretly. Each of us can sip a few alcoholic or nonalcoholic drinks alone without attracting the wrath of other members of our household, by not saying the kind of things we say for laughs over drinks.

Because I was not ready to be the source of my family scrutiny or face the false accusation of my cook and gardener, I kept the experience I narrated in the concluding paragraph of the previous chapter to myself. However, I decided to replicate a similar circumstance to the one that prompted the experience. *I will rule out coincidence if it happens again,* I reasoned. So, I sipped some Caribbean rum and stepped into my study the next day. Before opening my Bible, I prayed.

"Dear God, I know you live in my life. Kindly send your Holy Spirit to help me understand the Bible."

This time, I added a line I did not say in my first prayer about the Holy Spirit: "May you show me whether what happened before was a coincidence or something you planned — I have many questions to ask you, but I need to be sure that I was not hallucinating or tipsy from consuming alcohol."

As I opened the Bible, my scholarly instincts overwhelmed me. I employed my intellectual and analytical skills to read and to draw conclusions. After reading a couple of passages, I did not feel any difference. It was like a regular academic exercise.

However, as I prepared to close my reading session, I read through a page with information that amazed me. It said something to the effect that someone in a natural state of mind would be unable to receive what the Holy Spirit had to teach through the scriptures because one can only discern such things spiritually. In other words, the passage talked about the inspiration of the scriptures. Such inspiration was also about the work of the Spirit in me as I read the Bible. I opened to a couple more pages and read the prayer of Paul for the Ephesians. Apostle Paul prayed to God that the Ephesians would receive the spirit of wisdom and revelation in the knowledge of God. There and then, I understood the need for a direct relationship or one on one experience with God. Such a link can only work through the Holy Spirit, which abides in us. In short, the process requires knowing God (which each person will do for him or herself), not merely having knowledge about God.

Yes, I know God. As an African who has interacted with three generations of his family, I know God as my family did. I also know that my forefathers created their God and by extension, their religion. Yes, they did that out of fear. They could not understand or explain what made trees such as the Iroko to multiply exponentially in size and subsist for many years. They were unable to explain why lots of rivers and oceans surrounded them.

Also, they could not understand why certain things happened. So, they assembled under such trees and gathered by riverbanks to pay homage to whatever was responsible for such inexplicable occurrences. They also poured libations on the ground and invoked the spirits of their dead relatives for protection. By using oceans, trees, the land, and dead relatives among other things as intermediaries for reaching what was responsible for things they could not explain, my forefathers created the concept of God, which I was introduced to at puberty. Religion also emanated from the same practice, as a process for adhering to beliefs that regulated their behavior. Africans practiced a communication system where knowledge was received and preserved orally. In Africa, people use folktales and stories to transmit information orally from one generation to another. As such, there is no scripture or written document to attest that our forbears created God and religion, but they deserve some credit.

Having completed my reasoning, I was ready to leave my study, but an impression came to my heart that I knew God, but not the one created by my forefathers. I had invited the God of my student into my life. Also, I asked the Holy Spirit to come into my life. "The Spirit guides us into all truth," someone seems to say in my heart.

So, I paused, and the impression became intense. I am positive that my forefathers came up with the concept of

God in their brains. They used the power of their thoughts to create God, whatever God meant to them. Could this be a different God? About the God I invited into my life, *He is the way, truth, and life.* So, where is the Holy Spirit in all this? I pondered.

Humanity needs the Holy Spirit to teach them about Him.

This saying sounded strange, and then came another.

He did not create any religion. He created humankind to have a relationship with them, but humanity derailed. Thus, the first of Belief Literacy Steps should be to restore the relationship humanity lost from their maker or source.

"I respectfully disagree," I said out loud.

"Humanity, as we know it today, is a product of evolution. God created a man and afterward sensed that it was not suitable for the man to be alone. As such, He created a woman to be a companion for the man," I continued.

"The evolved man of today is different. While he needs companionship like the man you created, he does not always consider women most suitable for the company. The same applies to the evolved woman of today. She has found solace in persons of the same sex. The man and woman God created did not discriminate between each other along racial lines. The evolved men and women of today discriminate along racial lines. These people who have strayed from what God intended are experts in using their brains. Almost everything the changed people do today is a product of their thought patterns. Evolutionary people did not create things like mighty oceans and lousy weather, but they fabricated pieces of equipment to help them navigate the seas and harsh weather conditions. For example, when evolved people needed roads, they built bridges across the oceans You created. To show that our understanding of companionship has changed, we became lesbians, gays, bisexuals, and transgender people. The most-evolved among us are still questioning who they are. By the way, I am part of the evolved people, and we rely on our brain for solutions to our problems. Our evolution is the reason behind *Belief Literacy Steps*, which I anchor on our ability to think and use our minds."

The impression returned more gently.

He is the maker of humankind. He made them so they could have a relationship with Him, but they derailed. He gave humanity the brain on which you hinge Belief Literacy Steps. Choose and associate with whatever you consider an outcome of the human mind and see if it endures. After all, return and tell me if you would follow the maker of a product or the product of a maker? Also, see if you will agree that the first of Belief Literacy Steps should be to restore the lost relationship of humanity with their source or maker.

section three

CHAPTER 17

Skylife in the Minneapolis Skyway

You can overcome the fear of death by living in one of the best places in the United States of America.

My experiences with the Holy Spirit detailed in the previous chapters were like observations using the scientific method. I hypothesized that the Holy Spirit would visit anyone who invited God through prayer. This person would receive instructions through impressions that would often be inconsistent with rationality, which would make the recipient less likely to obey. Nevertheless, I decided to follow through with the directives of the impressions I received. The need to ascertain if a reliable product of human thought would fail me while on the verge of giving it all my trust prompted my decision. Thus, I decided I would get a job and live in a state in the north-central United States, an area called the Midwest. It would be an exciting adventure because I had lived and worked in the south-central region for many years. I never thought of doing a similar thing in the Midwest, because of their signature frightful winter weather. I did an excellent job avoiding anything that would make me work or reside anywhere with cold weather because I do not do well in the cold.

I got a job as planned, but after about a year of living in Nebraska, I did not see any human invention capable of disappointing me after I put my trust in it completely. I felt I should have seen something like that in the Midwest because of their weather. There should be something designed from a man's thinking to checkmate the excesses of nature around me, I reasoned. So, I asked my family members, coworkers, and friends for input. Someone suggested Minnesota.

"If what you are looking for relates to Midwest weather, it must be in Minnesota because their winter has it all," she said. Everyone I asked agreed. So, I decided to move further into the Midwest to explore what life would be like in Minnesota. However, I began to wonder how I would get a job that could propel my relocation to Minnesota.

As I drowned in my thoughts, I remembered that I embarked on this same adventure following my encounter with the Holy Spirit, so I prayed for direction. The new line I added to my prayer was, "Show me how to relocate to Minnesota." Unlike other times I prayed, I did not get an immediate impression, but I felt peace in my heart. The following day, as I was reading in my study, I felt the impression, and the following dialogue ensued.

"Will your brain and thought process allow you to relocate and live in Minnesota?"

"Nope," I said aloud, as if I was talking to someone physically present in my study.

"Why not?"

"Because of the cold weather," I replied.

"Do you believe you can live in Minnesota without worrying about the cold?"

"Impossible!" I exclaimed.

"Yes, you can live in one of the cities during the worst of winter without worrying about the cold."

"Please, show me how I can do this," I pleaded.

Two days later, I saw an advertisement. The Minnesota unit of the firm I worked for had an opening. The sad part was that there was only one available. My colleagues and I considered such an opportunity as someone else's promotion. As such, I was reluctant to apply for the job. Eventually, I summoned up the courage and applied for the position. After about two weeks, the hiring officials listed me as one of the most qualified applicants and recommended me for employment consideration. Within another two weeks, the hiring officials invited me for an interview. The email said I could interview over the phone, through video or in-person. I quickly repeated my prayer and added a new line, "Please, let me know the interview format to choose." This time, the impression came swiftly. I felt a deep urge to go for the in-person interview.

I replied to the email stating that I would be coming over for an in-person interview slated about a week ahead. About 13 days after the interview, they offered me the position. My office was located in downtown Minneapolis.

So, I reported for work three weeks later in August of 2018. The weather was beautiful, but there was nowhere to live. So, I checked into a hotel while I commenced my hunt for an apartment. After about a month, I moved into an apartment a few blocks away from my office. Something caught my attention – my office and my apartment were in the Minneapolis Skyway network. So, I began to live a sky-life, if there is such a thing. I went for weeks without getting to the street level of downtown Minneapolis. There were numerous shops where I purchased my necessities. A grocery store was two blocks away from my residence, linked to the Skyway. Because living the Sky-life was pure joy, I concluded that I was living in one of the best places anyone could live in the United States. As such, I was ready for death because I felt I had seen it all (not really prepared to die literally). Mind you, it was not my first time seeing or using a Skyway. I had seen some Skyways in many places in North America and others in a few countries in Europe, but I'd never had the opportunity to live and work on a continuous Skyway system that spanned many miles.

As I marveled at such a magnificent product of human thought, I began to pour accolades on humankind and how their brains and power to think led to such a barrier against the harshness of weather. As a newcomer, I missed my way several times in the Skyway. Although there were maps placed at strategic locations in the Skyway, I ignored them out of excitement. I also knew about apps to help navigate the Skyway, but I did not bother to download any of them because of my high sense of adventure. After about a week of missing my way, I figured out how to move back and forth between my apartment and my office. The months flew by faster than I had anticipated and then came the end of 2018 and start of 2019, with its attendant winter. I experienced horrible weather conditions with the temperature plummeting to less than negative 60 degrees at some point when frostbite occurred in about five minutes or less.

Surprisingly, it did not feel like winter to me. As a result, I did not buy a winter coat, gloves, jacket, thermal wear, or any of the stuff people who live in cold areas buy. On several occasions, I went shopping in shorts, a t-shirt, and a fez cap as if it were summer. That was because both my apartment and office were on the 7th floors of high-rise buildings linked to the Skyway. So, I watched it all from the comfort of my room or office. Sometimes I felt the cold, but not like someone at the street level would. One day my colleague Billy saw me walk into our office early in the morning and screamed at me.

"Where is your coat? Are you out of your mind? How can

you walk in the cold dressed that way?" he yelled, incredulous.

"I walked to the office from my apartment in the Skyway," I said casually.

"Really?" he asked and added, *"Lucky you."* On another occasion I met Arnold, another colleague, in the elevator. As the carriage shafted its way to our office floor, he looked at me and asked, *"Is this how you dress to work?"*

I said, *"Yes, because I live a few minutes away from here, in the Skyway."*

Smiling, he said, *"Nobody knows your commute."*

I had access to virtually everything I needed in the Skyway, from movie theaters and sports arenas, to my doctor's office, ophthalmologist, and dentist. Indeed, I was so comfortable living in the Skyway that most times I left my apartment without my wallet. I did so because life on the Skyway was predictable. I knew what to expect each day. I was also willing to walk back to my apartment if anything happened, or I needed something at home. I felt so comfortable, relaxed, and at home on the Skyway that I began to wonder why anyone would have any reason to doubt the capability of the human mind to think up appropriate solutions to social problems. Indeed, the Minneapolis Skyway provided a clear example that the human mind could achieve anything. One day, out of excitement, I yelled, "I put my trust in the Skyway because it is reliable."

Suddenly, I got that impression again, around January 30th, 2019.

He created all the raw materials that went into building what you admire this day. He created men and women and gave them the mental fortitude to think and make things. There are limitations to the human mind. Do not give glory to His creation. All glory belongs to Him. Instantly, I doubted the impression because I was convinced that the Skyway was a prime example of the extent of the power of a human brain.

The following day, at work, I received an email from the manager of our office building. It said that a portion of the Skyway by an apartment building close to our office was closed because of the freezing temperature, which caused significant damages to water pipes. The author of the email advised that anyone who planned to use the skyway would have to turn left at the apartment with a leaky pipeline and head to a bank building on the Skyway to navigate their way around the building. In the alternative, according to the email, one could also use the elevators to step outside the building and get back in the Skyway at the next building. It sounded like a nice gesture with simple and easy to follow instructions. I passed through that apartment building on my way to the office that morning and noticed that there was water in some places. I never knew they would eventually shut down that section of the Skyway. So, I did not bother to ask any further questions until I got off work in the evening. Upon arriving at the building with broken pipes, I had no need to think of what my next steps would be. Deciding on what to do next was a no brainer, even though I had no idea how to reach the location of the bank to walk around and return to my route on the skyway. Descending the steps to the street level and joining the skyway through the next building was not an option for me. The reason was that I wore my usual attire: a blazer, chino pants, and casual shoes. There was nothing about my attire that suggested I was in Minnesota, and it was about negative 15 degrees outside. I was dressed like someone attending a business meeting in the middle of summer in Florida. Indeed, I was not worried about the weather at all.

Why should I have worried? My dressing reflected the same way I had dressed since my arrival in Minneapolis in August of the previous year. I never went to the downtown street level. I was always at the Sky level, even when I had to drive out. I connected the car park through the Skyway. I would later learn the hard way that it was the last day of a two-day, record-breaking cold that forced Minnesotans to close businesses, offices, and schools in the entire state. So, I turned left in the hopes of getting to the bank building and walking around the building with broken pipes.

After almost an hour of walking, I found myself on the verge of stepping into what looked like a stadium. I became confused. I did not know that the skyway was that massive. I had never even seen that section of the Skyway. I began to wonder why some people woke up one morning and closed their part of the skyway because of some broken pipes. Why did they wait for the pipes to break? Could they not have done some repair work on those pipes before then? Why did they not put up a sign to direct a newcomer on how to locate the place to begin to walk around? At precisely that moment, I realized that I was lost. So, I brought out my cell phone and began to ask myself, "Is this an emergency? How will whoever is coming to get me know my location?"

I could see the street, but going outside was not an option. I would die from frostbite if I stepped out!

Helplessly, I repeated my prayer and added a new line. "Please, forgive me. I have trusted a product of the human brain instead of the maker or source of the human mind. Please, take me back to my apartment without any incident or embarrassment. I do not want to call 911 for help because I look stupid for dressing like a man who sees summer in the winter."

After the prayer, I looked to my right and saw a gentleman. I would later learn of his kindness and exchange telephone numbers with him, as well as learn that his name is Josh.

"Excuse me, sir. I am lost. I am new in Minneapolis. Please, help me." I begged desperately.

"Where are you going?" he asked.

I told him the name of my apartment. So, we located the nearest map to search for how to get to my place. We found my residence on the map, but he told me that I was more than 45 minutes away from home.

"Let us go to the street level and join a bus, so I show you where to stop," he said.

"Nope," I replied. "See the way I am dressed, no coat, no gloves, and no jacket." He looked at me, puzzled, and brought out a cell phone. He pulled up an app that had a map and told me to follow him. We walked for almost an hour before we reached a location where I screamed, "Josh, I know here! I walk past here every morning to my office. I have shopped at the stores around here many times. I, therefore, can find my way back to my apartment from here."

I walked him back a few steps and told him that I did not want to be lost again, so he continued alone. I got to my apartment 10 minutes later and sent him a text message asking his whereabouts. He replied that he entered a train safely and was on his way to a city in the suburbs, where he lived, far away from downtown Minneapolis.

Knowing that Josh was safely on his way home, I dashed into a store two blocks away and bought a coat, some gloves, a jacket, and a set of thermal wear. When I returned to my apartment, I began to reflect on what transpired. Perhaps, this impression I kept getting was right. Because He created humankind and gave them brains, it may not be proper for us to be overly dependent on our minds. Maybe we should depend, not on our minds, but the creator of our minds. As such, I am tempted to conclude that anyone who invites God into his or her life through prayer will receive visitation from the Holy Spirit. Such a person will also receive instructions through impressions that may appear inconsistent with rationality, which makes the recipient less likely to obey. Nevertheless, those instructions are troves of treasures one can only discover through obedience.

CHAPTER 18

Wow. Someone Understands!

Most times it does not look like it, but God understands everything about the world and the circumstances surrounding its inhabitants.

*A*fter the Skyway experience, I began to have an internal dialogue. I thought I was losing my mind.

"What you call impressions are not impressions," I always seemed to hear.

"Excuse me, but I say what I think *you* mean, or what is going on in *my* mind as a result of my experiences. Do you have a different meaning or expression for these impressions?" I'd often retaliate.

"You are hearing from a Person, the Holy Spirit, not a feeling. The Holy Spirit is part of the Trinity who understands you and your concerns," the voice would reply.

"*Wow, does someone understand?*" I queried.

"Yes, but I can leave if you do not want me. Do you want me?"

"Yes, I need you. Please, do not go away." I responded.

"I have been hovering over you for many years, but you have not received me. You received me only when you invited me, after meeting with your student, but I keep hovering because your heart has not entirely yielded to my leading."

"Thank you for disclosing that to me. I apologize. I will yield to your leading from now on."

"So, where does the Spirit fit in the dynamics of belief literacy?" I asked.

"You are anchoring your understanding of belief on human senses, but unfortunately, the Father did not create men and women to live by their senses. What you do not see, hear, feel, taste, or touch is more real than what you see, hear, feel, taste, or touch. As such, you should revisit your premise and follow me as I lead."

"Okay," I said. Then I continued, "I want to follow the leading of the Holy Spirit, but I am not oblivious to the fact that I live in a dangerous time in history. Because of events of the recent past and what is happening, I know I live in an epoch that may not be smart to identify as a Christian. Some of the Christian clergies I know in the United States are hypocrites. They condemn people openly for their sexual orientation while sexually abusing innocent boys and girls in secret. Christian preachers are also preying on and exploiting the poor. In Nigeria, for example, poor Christians slave their lives away to make money to donate to churches for building high-end educational institutions. When such schools are ready, these poor

Christians watch agape as they are unable to afford tuition for their children and wards into the schools they built with their blood, sweat, and tears. Also, I have noticed that churchgoers, all over the world, are like my grandparents, great grandparents and their ancestors, who were afraid and ignorant. I say so because they embrace religion as a means of escaping reality. I have also noticed the same ignorance in members of other religious groups."

"Quit whining," was the impression that came to my heart.

"You are lamenting about religion, whereas I am referring to a relationship. Get your Bible, so I can direct you to His word."

"The Bible? But isn't the Bible religion?" I asked skeptically.

"Yes, but the Bible is not an instrument of capitalism, like you thought. The Bible has historically accurate information that will be of interest to you. The Bible contains His words, which is not for a time, but for ages past, present, and to come. Although you do not like what it says about the man who has little because according to you, he became a victim of appropriation for the benefit of the man who has more, it was a parable meant to teach about a more profound truth. The parable shows how He endowed everyone with abilities. It also shows the need for obedience and the consequence of disobedience. *The missionaries who used the Bible for political domination were Christians. Unfortunately, the Bible is not a Christian book. A political figure may have authorized the translation you talked*

about, but the Bible is not political. The Bible is a legal book that contains my laws. It also embodies the covenant God has with His creation. Those who embark on same-sex sexual acts have turned away from God. Such people engage in sexual immoralities and will not inherit the kingdom of God. The law that says thou shall not steal should remind you about the importance of laws. Now, anchor Belief Literacy Steps on laws because men and women will live purposefully fulfilled lives only when they follow appropriate laws."

Shocked by the above, I repeated my usual prayers with a new line: "Please, Holy Spirit, teach me the Bible, show me the entire Bible so I can see how the laws of God should be the foundation of Belief Literacy Steps." To my consternation, I found that the Bible contained credible answers to all the things that confused me about life. In the following chapters, I will share some of the things I learned from studying the Bible while I lived in near-solitude. The knowledge I apportion in upcoming chapters makes me want to call what is in preceding chapters "fake news" because it seems like the real deal is about to unfold. However, there is a caveat. There are some prerequisites to observe. In order to embrace the knowledge I am proposing, we have to first accept that God created us and that God is in charge of human affairs on earth. We should also believe that we are descendants of Adam and Eve, the first couple who disobeyed God. It was their disobedience that broke our relationship with

God. We also must accept that the rebellion of Adam and Eve has made you and I sinners and we can neither save nor help ourselves.

Additionally, we should acknowledge that we humans are not yet where we should be in life as a consequence of the first couple's disobedience. Due to the inherent nature of love, God did not give up on humanity. Instead, God sent Jesus Christ, His only begotten son, to come and atone for our sins with His life. Finally, we should understand that anyone who confesses God's son, Jesus, as his or her Lord and personal savior as well as believes in Him, will receive salvation. Mind you that there are multiple dimensions to salvation. Being well-educated or financially well-to-do does not preclude you from the need for salvation. After admitting and proclaiming that He is Lord, we should begin to abide in His laws, a process that reunites us with God, our source. With such reunification in place, we will realize that God created us and kept us on Earth for specific reasons, which include taking charge of the planet. After observing the above prerequisites, you are ready to progress to the next chapter. It is also important to note that your religious affiliation or detachment is inconsequential because you are about to embark on a personal journey to transform your life.

CHAPTER 19

The Kingdom View of the Literacy of Belief

In spite of our distance from God, we can reconnect with Him and lead a meaningful life from today.

I have often questioned why God is involved in the affairs of humankind in spite of the scientific advancements we have made. I also wondered why humans have not outgrown God. However, having studied the mind of God as documented in the Bible, it is illuminating to say that answers abound to the multiplicity of questions that bug many freethinkers, including myself. Humans cannot outgrow God. An attempt to grow too big for God would be in the same class as a fruit tree in a garden, trying to abandon the person who planted it. This tree is embarking on an exercise in futility. Life would be a meaningless adventure for humanity without God. The planter of a fruit tree cannot stop the tree from growing as tall as the tree wants to grow, but he or she can always bend the tree or climb it to harvest the fruits. The word of God, as documented in the Bible, emphasizes that *all of humanity is yearning for freedom*. Perhaps, that explains why we ask a multiplicity of questions.

In line with the plans of God, Jesus Christ has set us free by bearing our sins through His death, resurrection, and ascension into Heaven. As a result, true freedom comes from restoring our relationship with Him. Such restoration paves the way for us to obtain the freedom of the glory reserved for children of God through Christ. As such, I have seen that it is tough for humans to outgrow God because they cannot proceed in life without Him.

I also know that God is a constant part of the activities of men and women because the world belongs to Him. He is present and a part of everyone who lives in the world. Because of His loving nature, He does not allow us to wander in the world. He gives us His word to guide and direct our footsteps. The word of God is more significant than English, an imperialistic language through which most of us read the Bible.

Before now, I viewed the Bible as a colonial artifact because I thought it was imposed on my forefathers, but I was wrong. Although the people who used the Bible for selfish ends succeeded in deceiving my people to give up all they had, the Bible is not an instrument of oppression or colonization. Besides, I now know that those missionaries cum businessmen and politicians who vandalized

Africa did not live the lifestyle of King Jesus Christ, as shown in the Bible. They were religious people who were not as loving as the King encouraged us to be. They were also members of the Christian religion, but I now know that the Bible is not a Christian book. That is why I forgave them. I want to be like the King and have His kind of heart.

He prayed that His father should forgive those who would later kill Him. As religious people, like Christians, persecuted Him, He remained kind to them. As they nailed Him, a King, to a cross, He prayed for them. He asked His Father to forgive them, regardless of what they did because from His point of view they did not know what they were doing. Does this mean that God is all about being merciful? Nope. He is also a consuming fire, but He grants us His grace to return to Him for restoration. I often compare His window period to building credit in the United States. It is an odd comparison, but it helped me to understand the importance of His grace and the consequences of delay. Your lender or credit card company provides you with a due date so you can make your payments. If you miss the due date, they will give you some more time to make the payment. If you still do not make the payment, they will add late fees. If you fail to make your payment, they will send your account to a collection agency. You can pay off the debt, including more charges the agency will add within a specified period, or you make a payment arrangement. If you continue to fail to make the payment, the agency will slam the information on your credit report as derogatory.

With derogatory items on your credit file, it becomes tough to get credit. What if I pay cash? Yes, you can, if you have the money. Such derogatory information also has a snowball effect in that it negatively affects other areas of your life like employment, buying a home, and obtaining funds for education. Can't I file bankruptcy? Yes, you can, but it depends on whether or not you are an individual or a corporate entity. While bankruptcy may reduce or eliminate the debts, it may further damage your credit history. However, the passage of time has a way of reducing the impact of the derogatory information in your credit history. After a certain period you can receive the same things people with excellent credit get, including becoming the president of the United States, after multiple bankruptcies.

Missing your payment is like sinning. The trauma you get from those incessant phone calls as collection agents attempt to recover what you owe is like the challenges we face in life after disconnecting ourselves from our source. The waiting period they give you to make your payment and the fact that even after bankruptcy, which is the height of delinquency, you can still purchase what other people with good credit can buy or even surpass them reminds me of the grace of God. Mind you that grace does not cancel the law. Grace enables us to fulfill the requirements. The grace we receive from Jesus Christ enables us to follow Him. Nevertheless, God is a consuming fire. He is also a just father who holds everyone accountable to the same standards. Sin is an abomination unto God, and it has far more consequences than missing a credit card payment. The Bible makes it clear that sin results in death, but we often interpret it as the end of our physical bodies. As such, when we sin on a Monday and have not died by Tuesday, we assume sin does not have any consequence. Unfortunately, we do not understand that God's wrath will eventually come from heaven against all sinners.

The misery and suffering confronting humanity today should remind us of the effect of our sins. There is now a sinking degradation of human thinking and behavior. Humankind seems to have lost track of what it means to be human. For example, some people are now justifying their quest to change their at-birth sexual identity to whatever they want. Some male individuals no longer understand what it means to be a man. As such, we see a prevalence of homosexuality. Some women are also part of the confusion. Men and women no longer depend on each other for survival. Indeed, human society is growing more individualistic. The most disgusting aspect is that most people do not know that we came to planet Earth from a source and for a purpose, and that until we reconnect with our source, our lives will remain in shambles. We should also understand that Jesus Christ rules our world from heaven.

As our King, He wants us to reap the full benefits of His Kingdom. He wants our lives to reflect the riches and glory of Heaven. Such understanding is the key to steering our minds to our desired destination. Let us now revisit *Belief Literacy Steps* for those who understand the need to live a purposeful life by God's Kingdom principles.

Identify Yourself

If you have ever taken an examination outside a formal school environment, then you have experienced what it is like to identify yourself. You will recall that the organizers of the test often verify your identity before they admit you into the testing center. People who have traveled outside their countries of birth, nationality, residence, or citizenship have also experienced what it is like to identify oneself. In these two scenarios, you are often expected to have some form of documentation that clearly states who you are. Such paperwork may range from a state or military-issued identity card to a driver's license, passport, or another government-issued form of identification. Those documentary evidence spur confidence in you. Indeed, knowing that you have something on your person to corroborate whatever you claim as your identity boosts your confidence. The assurance or courage you have, knowing that you have what is required to identify yourself, is a part of what steers your mind to better outcomes. In the case of an examination, you will be in the right frame of mind, knowing that you have been admitted to at least sit for the test.

If you have had an encounter with members of law enforcement in a foreign country without anything to prove your identity, then you are likely aware of the awkward and uncomfortable nature of such an experience. If you have observed the prerequisites listed in the previous chapter, your first Belief Literacy step to steering your mind toward achieving your desire is to identify yourself. However, you cannot identify yourself without knowing who you are. Before they showed their identification documents, the test taker and traveler above knew who they were. The act of knowing yourself is like the Biblical injunction for citizens of the kingdom of God to be separate from the world. Other members of the world struggle to understand their identity. As such, being different is necessary to achieve any reasonable thing you desire in life, but first things first, you have to grasp your status in the world with the almighty God.

We are God's image because God brought us out from Himself, which explains why He often wonders aloud if we know that we are gods. Although we have physical parents, God is our spiritual father. He created us so He can have a relationship and fellowship with us.

The type of association and relationship God wants to

have with us is not the kind created by man, like what exists between rich and poor countries (which led to what we call the north-south dichotomy). Such man-made arrangement is a political, socioeconomic conceptualization, which reminds us of the unequal exchange existing among countries. It is not like a country being a member of a world body with equal vote as others, yet a few privileged countries among them belong to an inner caucus that decides who gets what, when, and how. Humankind should have a father-child relationship with God where the child receives love from his or her father. Some of my students often misunderstand fatherhood because of the shift in societal perception of parenthood, or because they have not had any association with their biological fathers.

Hopefully, some people still remember that a father is a real man and that a real man takes care of his offspring. A real man does not just deposit his sperm and run away. He comes back to check on that boy or girl who has become a part of him even if he disagrees with the woman who birthed the child. He calls, visits, and supports his child or children because a father's love is unending. Similarly, humankind was made to be recipients of all the love and grace of God because He is our father and our source.

Because God is a Spirit, the men and women He created are also Spirits. No wonder he mandated us to worship Him only in spirit and in truth. His spiritual nature is not meant to scare us because it does not diminish the fact that He is our Papa. Fathers do not scare their children away. Sometimes children may see their father as mean or talkative, but it does not stop them from wholly trusting in his capacity to provide for their needs. Perhaps, that explains why your kids never wonder if you are broke or not in a good mood when they ask for something. They ask unconsciously, believing that you will provide for them because you are their father. They ask because you are their source and provider. Once you identify and understand your identity, you position yourself to take the next step in the *Literacy of Belief*.

Evaluate your Identity

Before showing an authority figure his or her identification, our exam taker and traveler evaluated their identification documents. Are my driver's license, identity card, or passport expired? What type of material is valid for identifying myself to the requester? Is there a significant change in my appearance compared to my picture on the document identifying me? These are some of the questions that helped them to evaluate themselves before asserting the authority that is inherent in their identity. Our lives are intended to showcase the attributes of God because He created us in His image and likeness. Thus, we should always ask questions such as *"Am I manifesting His characteristics?"* To display His qualities, we should fellowship with Him and make soul-winning our priority, among other factors. As we fellowship with God and win souls, we share in His authority. Another question we should ask is, *"Am I sharing in His administration?"* Because God is not selfish, he gave us dominion over other elements of His creation. As such, we should also ask, *"Is what He created dominating me?"* If you are addicted to some drugs originating from leaves, it means that God's creation is dominating you. If you are asking God to give you money or help to pay your bills, you are also an example of some-one dominated by God's creation. He created things you can put together to get what you want. As a result, it is amusing to ask God for money when He has promised to bless the work of your hands. Will He find you doing any-thing He can bless? His blessings will translate into cash for you. In the absence of work, there will not be anything to bless. Under such a circumstance, you will continue to pray in vain because you are asking for the wrong thing.

Enter the big one! Are we obeying His laws? Also, evaluate your identity in light of what He told Joshua. God encouraged Joshua to ensure that the book of the law did not depart from his mouth. We should meditate on His precepts day and night and abide by the same. If you an-swered three *yeses* and a *no* to all the evaluation questions listed above, you are most likely sharing in His adminis-tration by working with Him to restore humanity to His purpose. As such, you are ready for the final step.

Take Action

The required action in this final step is ironic because it is like taking action steps while standing. However, this action is the most significant advantage of being a child of God. *Cast your burdens on Me*, He says. Because we work with Him in our vineyard and have made soul-winning our priority, we should not worry about anything else. Surprisingly, that is the action you should take: *not worrying about anything*. However, such action does not mean that one should fold his or her arms and wait for food to drop from the sky. He made food to flow on humanity from the air only once, and has since then learned His lessons. Kingdom citizens are not to worry about what to eat or drink because their heavenly father knows about their needs. We should first and foremost seek His kingdom and righteousness, so He can give us everything else we need. Nonkingdom citizens are those who ought to run after or worry about their daily needs.

As believers, we should not doubt God's ability to provide for us. Sometimes, we become discouraged because we are not always aware of the processes involved as He provides for us.

However, He gives us His provision by ordering our steps, giving us peace, guiding the right people our way, and giving us access to His unlimited resources. It is vital for us to ask Him through prayer to order our steps because we cannot go far on our own. We need Him to order and guide our actions, especially because many ways seem right to us, but they are paths to destruction. Also, it is not the duty of Kingdom men and women to order their steps. Can someone who is taking action also order his or her steps? We need the Lord to order our steps daily. As soon as we surrender our ways and allow Him to take charge, we will have the peace that passes all understanding. Do you remember the tree-branch comparison in the Bible? Jesus compares Himself to a tree and tells us that we are the branches while God, our father, is the husbandman. With this analogy, we see the need for us to associate with Him because we will not accomplish much outside of Him.

Because of our connection to Him, our chances of being involved in the right relationships with the right people increase. Being connected to people and maintaining the right relationships matters to Him. It helps in fulfilling His principle that if any two of us shall agree about anything in His name, He will do it for us. Also, He will fulfill the promise of His presence anywhere two or three of us gather in His name. Finally, we should remember that He will supply all our needs according to His riches in glory. We also have to work, and our work should be in line with His purpose. We should not put round pegs in square holes as we work. He gave each of us a variety of gifts, which we should discover and link to His work.

To determine your purpose and endowments, you

need to figure out what you are willing to do even without compensation, or what comes to you naturally. Jesus told us that those who worked their lands would have an abundance. I became excited because He said I could do all things through Him. To do implies action, which explains why He said that those whose hands are diligent will rule whereas lazy ones will end up in forced labor. In other words, everyone will eventually work (or take action); those who are diligent will become rulers over the lazy ones who will also work, but by force.

In conclusion, the third step of the revised *Belief Literacy Steps* is to take actions of faith and put our trust in Him. With certainty, God will supply all our needs according to His riches in glory as we work in alignment with His purpose. We should always remember His promise to provide for us when we ask. He also said that we will find when we seek. He will open every necessary door because He is our father, and fathers do not give their children stones when they ask for candy.

CHAPTER 20

Does Fear Fuel Every Belief?

Most times we erroneously believe that fear fuels every human quest for the supernatural.

*T*hese days I reflect on the various belief systems I have explored. I am often tempted to view fear as the central element that prompts people to adhere or subscribe to belief systems. Such view stems from a series of encounters I have had with individuals who build upon and advocate ideas that consist of deities and idols. I now know that when humankind has faith in the potency of such phenomena and propagate a belief in them, they develop fear in their objective consciousness. Such fear comes because people do not entirely understand what they believe. Enveloped in fear of an unclear belief system, people often become victims of circumstances of their own making. Such reasoning explains why it is vital for humankind to connect with their creator. Connecting with your source is like returning home. For everyone, there is a place to call home, a place of security where we are sure of finding love. Home is where we know someone cares for and respects us. It brings memories of unquestioning trust and compassion. Home reminds us of an excellent place of beginning, not where life ends. Home is a safe place, so reliable that we are not afraid to make mistakes. Most importantly, the right home environment offers us a full-service launchpad that provides us access to the necessary platforms of life.

Such a launchpad is what we receive when we restore our relationship with God, our creator, through His Son Jesus Christ. Belief in Him is fueled by necessity, not fear, because our home is in Him. Jesus is the only one with open and inviting hands that are ready to welcome those who long for inner peace and fulfillment in life. It is also essential to note that your native language may have different names or designations for God and Jesus Christ, but there is a clear, uniform set of experiences that come to those who are genuinely seeking Him. Another point to note is that our brain is inherently unreliable as we take significant steps in life.

He provides a foolproof method for us to extract answers to the questions that bug us daily. Out of love and care for us, God sacrificed His only begotten Son so we could have everlasting life. We should trust Him so He will fulfill the desires of our hearts. The Bible contains His infallible word, and there is a clear and compelling path by which we can network with Him. That path is known as prayer. Yes, we can talk to Him through prayer, which is a crucial component of our walk with Him.

The Bible recorded many great things Jesus did during His time on Earth. It is ironic that out of all the great things He did, His disciples prioritized prayer and asked Him to share with them how to pray. Had I been in their shoes, I would have asked Him to show me how to do much more than pray. I would plead for more, but on second thought, I realize that prayer was the secret behind His significant accomplishments. To position ourselves for strategic exploits in life, we need to understand more about prayers. I believe that prayer is a communication line that links us from the world (where God gave us to control) to heaven (where God lives and manages). God created humankind to be in charge of the physical world, while He remains in charge of the heavenly domain. If for any reason we need God to intervene from His area of jurisdiction to ours, we should invite Him through prayer. As we pray, we give God the legal authority to influence our physical domain – the world – because we are the ones He gave all legal authority over the physical world. As such, the ability to pray is a foundational requirement for those who desire to take *Belief Literacy Steps* successfully. Does God answer prayers? Yes, He does. Jesus will answer our prayers and grant our requests because His heart is full of compassion. He even grants the needs of the confused.

By confused, I am referring to those who are unable to articulate their needs accurately.

For instance, Jesus once asked a man if he wanted Him to heal him. Instead of just saying yes, the man began to whine and took Jesus down Pity-Me-Avenue.

"Sir, my family members have abandoned me and now that I am on the river bank I do not have anyone to take me into the river when the angel troubles the water," said the confused man.

As if He did not hear him, Jesus told him to pack his sleeping bag and leave because He had already healed him. Do you have doubts about how compassionate He is? Well, expel those misgivings. At some point, a man who had leprosy met Him and said something to the effect that Jesus could heal him if it were His will.

Contrary to the man's reasoning, Jesus had compassion on the leper and healed him. He understands our pains. He knows how tough things are for humanity because He once resided on Earth as a human. I have prayed and received answers many times. I also know that unanswered prayers are capable of discouraging believers in their walk with the Lord. Such circumstances may even lead people to question God's integrity and power. I once thought that prayers were unanswered when we were not in a right relationship with God. However, I found that no one starts out in a right relationship with Him because we were conceived in sin. Perhaps, that is why He reassures us that whatever we ask in prayer, believing that we have already received, will be ours. However, we have to pray according to the principles of God's word.

Nevertheless, you should strive to be in a right relationship with God because sin is an abomination unto Him. But, and a big but, how best should one pray? We are not alone in wondering the best way to pray. His disciples also wondered along that direction, and eventually, they asked Him to teach them how to pray. In response, He taught them the famous *Our Lord's Prayer*, a prayer model most of us know by heart.

Before we dissect His prayer sample, it is essential to note that we should not come to Him in prayer because of what we expect to receive from Him. When we go to Him in such a manner, it resembles a one-sided relationship based on benefits. We should have a genuine and sincere love for Him as we pray and obey Him, and not follow Him because of what we want to gain from Him. To buttress my point, we should remind ourselves about His directive, that we love the Lord our God with all our hearts and with our souls and minds. He did not stop at that. He also reaffirmed that we should obey His commands if we love Him. Coming to Him in obedience puts our attitude into perspective. In what manner do we approach God in prayer? Do we come to Him out of love, obedience, and respect? Are we approaching Him, fully aware that He is holy? And, that we should not come to Him with sin in our hearts? Have we explored the cleansing power of His blood? Are we coming to him with hearts filled with praise to honor and worship Him? Have we separated ourselves from the stack?

Do we also believe? Do we have faith that He is the only One who can steer our hearts to achieve what we want to accomplish in life? In the final analysis, do our lives reflect His nature? If we can answer all these questions in the affirmative, then it is time to start behaving like our father by speaking things into reality. From childhood, I have heard that God spoke words, and that all the things He spoke about came into existence, including the world. He said let there be this and let there be that, and eventually, all the this and that came to be. However, I did not fully have a grasp of the power of the spoken word until I earned a doctorate in literacy. The term literacy is a fancy word for addressing our capability to encode and decode words as well as measure our knowledge. Thanks to my doctoral training, I now know that words are the foundation of knowledge. Learning is anchored on words because the words you speak are among the factors that determine if you will understand what the teacher is teaching. To my surprise, my training exposed me to how the words we speak affect our thinking process, as well as the actions we take in life.

It is therefore not strange for me to read in the Bible that His word is the beacon upon which the world stands.

In order words, God spoke the world into existence. He continues to talk to this day. As such, we should mirror Him and express our desires into action through prayers. We should start talking about what we have asked of Him in prayer as if it is already in existence. What we say reflects what we believe in our hearts. The good news is that God has given us a power similar to the one He uses to cause things to happen once He speaks. When and how did He give us this authority? He gave us the authority during creation by making us in His image and likeness. Have you ever looked into a mirror? I bet you saw yourself. This is also God's image. Whatever you see in the mirror as you look represents the image of God.

Similarly, when God looks into a mirror, He sees us. Indeed, what we speak is the word of faith, which we should continue to speak until we see the physical manifestation of our words. God has the power to create, which comes out of His mouth. When He made us for His glory, he extended a similar ability or power to us. So, we have to say our words with faith.

Faith is the evidence of what we do not see. It is an expression of our belief. In short, faith is our belief in action. We become what we believe through faith, which explains why people use belief and faith interchangeably. In effect, we have to believe the things we say even when they have not happened. We should believe until we start to behave as if what we believed is happening.

Mind you that this is not about positive confession. We are talking about a God-kind-of-faith disclosure. It is due to our faith in God. We confess because we believe in God. We pray because God answers prayers. The need to feed our minds with His words is of utmost importance because that is how faith comes. We should watch what goes into our ears and what we see because they are part of the gates to our hearts. Everything in life comes through His word, which is near us, in our mouths and hearts. Remember that whatever is in our hearts comes out of our mouths and our behavioral disposition.

Thus, we should ensure that what we say aligns with His word. For example, He said we should say we are strong when we are weak. Similarly, when we lack, we should say that we have, which shows that we believe He is capable of supplying our needs according to His riches in glory in Heaven. We cannot overemphasize the impact of what we believe, think, or say because they can affect us, negatively or positively. Such an effect will also reflect on our prayers. You cannot pray for one thing and start confessing the other. You will get the other, which you acknowledged through confession.

CHAPTER 21

Dissecting His Prayer Model

Prayer is a decisive component of belief.

The fact that He made out time to pray is a point that will feature prominently in my endeavor to examine the prayer life of our Lord and Savior, Jesus Christ. However, it must be noted that He did not pray out of compulsion or problems that confronted Him. Jesus put so much time in prayers because praying was a part of Him. Also, prayers took Him away for so long that His disciples wondered where He was. By so doing, He has given us prayer as a cardinal principle of Kingdom life to emulate. As such, praying is not an activity we should engage in only some-times. Prayer is something we should do at all times. As a teacher, I meditate on my lesson plans and notes. Doing this helps me to internalize my instructional objectives and appropriate delivery strategy for instruction.

In class, I use my utterances to show my students that

I meditated on and internalized the contents being taught in class. The things I say also put me on the right pedestal to teach my students multiple ways to enhance their choice-making process. I call what I do in class righteous teacher's activity because my intentions are genuine and sincere. I am also aware that my smart and exceptional students continue to reflect on what we discussed in class days, weeks, and months later.

The activities described above remind me of prayer because someone who prays engages in all of them. Yes, calling on the name of the Lord is akin to engaging in useful activity; to uttering, meditating, and reflecting. Indeed, prayer congregates actions, thoughts, words, and reflection under one roof. A teacher-student relationship also reminds me of our relationship with God.

A teacher who understands his or her craft knows that teaching is about playing a facilitatory role. Such a teacher does not compel students to follow his or her own point of view. The teacher lays out all the options in the learning environment so the students can have a multiplicity of opportunities to boost their power of choice. Such an arrangement is similar to what we share with our Father and King. Our Lord does not impose His will on us. He knows our needs. Indeed, before our mothers conceived us, He knew what our needs would be, yet He directed us to ask, seek, and knock. He even put life and death before us with a need to choose but insisted that we do the choosing. He is so abundant in mercy that He modeled how to talk to Him through prayers.

I have summarized His prayer model using the acronym SOV-R2-P4, which means Sovereignty, two words that begin with the letter R (Request and Remission), and four words that have P as their first letter. Those four words are Provision, Power, Praise, and Praise. *Our father, who is in Heaven* reminds us of God's sovereignty. He is the sovereign and supreme ruler of the Kingdom of Heaven. We should declare our loyalty and tell Him that His name is exceptional and of utmost significance in our lives. It is also imperative that we request for His will to take preeminence on Earth, which we can liken to our lives or the lives of those for whom we pray. Because we depend on Him for provision, we should implore Him to provide for us. There is also a need for us to ask Him to forgive us of our sins. We should remember to strive towards righteousness. As such, we must plead the precious blood of His only begotten Son for the remission of our sins, so we can have the appropriate framework to demand what is legitimately ours. We should inform Him that we also forgave those who wronged us. The power to walk in His faith and overcome sin comes from Him. As such, we should also ask Him to empower us. Finally, we have to praise Him because to Him are all praises due. Praise is doubled intentionally to help us to understand how important it is for us to adore His name through praises.

We also have to be like Jesus by observing some solitude and reverencing His name in prayer. Remember that we ought to pray when possible in a manner that will isolate us from distractions, so our father, who watches in secret, will reward us. We should come to him with deep respect as we confess our sins, which He will forgive because He is faithful and just. Indeed, we have to admit our sins as well as repent from them and not harbor any plan of returning to our sinful nature. It is also important to thank God as we make our requests known to Him. We should also be specific in our petition, while reminding God about His promises, as we plead our case with a grateful heart. Each of these stages requires that we believe and have the faith that He will do all we ask of Him. Thus, we should be in an anticipatory mood as we wait for His manifestation. Be that as it may, I believe we should understand that Jesus did not intend His prayer-model to be a ritualistic prayer for recitations. Let us see His model only as an example of how to pray.

As such, we should adapt the prayer to suit our circumstances. It is important to note that Jesus behaved much like an ordinary human being during His time on earth. He hardly tapped from His divine source. When circumstances confronted Him, He would exit the situation to pray. His attitude goes to show that prayer is something that replenishes and reinvigorates us. It is a very potent weapon provided by God for which humanity should be grateful. Jesus valued prayer so much that His attitude towards prayer should remind us that we are probably selling ourselves short. Yes, we underestimate ourselves by not making prayer a part of our lives. Thus, it is time for us to stop and to retrace our steps so we can incorporate prayer into our daily activities. God is ready to work with us in accomplishing His purpose if we make ourselves available and communicate with Him through prayer.

Examples of Answered Prayers

Because I am a victim of education, so to speak, I went in search of evidence of answered prayers. Yes, I consider myself a victim of formal education. I say so because Western education appears to have injured the way I think. Somehow, all the academic training I have acquired succeeded in making me a casualty of learning. Indeed, I am a victim of the learning method imposed on me by the educational systems I have encountered over the years. As such, I unconsciously subscribe to doctrines and strategies for the organized search for knowledge. Without giving it any thought, I want this search to involve the identification and formulation of problems and the collection of data through observation and experimentation before I make inferences. Also, I instinctively strive to engage in the formulation and testing of my assumptions or suppositions before drawing a conclusion. Such an approach to knowledge is in sharp contrast with everything prayer represents.

So, despite the Holy Spirit's guidance, I proceeded to subject prayer to some teacher examination. I hoped to find out whether I was alone in perceiving prayer as helpful and if other individuals would say that prayer also worked for them. By prayer working for them, I mean that such people would say they had such and such problems and that upon praying about the issues in the name of Jesus they received answers. Because prayer borders primarily on belief, I knew it would be complicated to subject my inquiry into complete scientific investigation. Although it was not impossible, I could not afford the necessary resources for conducting such a study. As such, the cost was the first limitation of my teacher examination of prayer. So, I engaged in what you may call a part quantitative and part qualitative inquiry into prayer aimed at understanding the perspectives of other human beings regarding prayer. Precisely, I needed to know if some people had had prayer-related experiences and what their outcomes were.

I asked 2500 people from 10 cities in three continents questions about their encounter with prayer using questionnaires and in-depth interviews. These people did not constitute what is known as a representative sample in research. However, they qualified for what you may call a convenient or opportunity sample. I choose them from among my relatives, friends, and acquaintances. They also recommended that I ask their friends, relatives of their friends, and their acquaintances whom they believed had some experiences with prayer. All the people I interviewed lived in the following cities: Gaborone in Botswana, Johannesburg in South Africa, Abuja, Lagos, and Onitsha in Nigeria. Others were from Amsterdam in the Netherlands, Lincoln in Nebraska, Minneapolis in Minnesota, Dubai in the United Arab Emirates, Tokyo in Japan, Dallas, and Houston in Texas. Of all the people, I spoke with 950 and distributed survey instruments to the rest. In response to the question about praying with others or being a part of any group that subscribes to prayer, all the people answered in the affirmative as well as listed the names of various Christian groups in the research questionnaires.

While those who indicated they have or had an affiliation with organizations that subscribe to prayer also reported having prayed through the name of our Lord and Savior Jesus Christ, others differed. Some identified themselves as African traditionalists, Muslims, Hindus, or persons without any religious affiliation. In spite of not identifying with organizations in tandem with the Christian faith, they acknowledged that they also prayed through the name of Jesus and subscribed to His Kingship and Lordship. As such, their prayers were answered because they prayed in the name of Jesus, but they did not consider themselves religious people. As strange as it sounded to my ears, the lesson was that anyone who confesses Jesus Christ as his or her personal Savior will receive His blessings. In regard to problems that were solved after prayers, participants listed many problems, including raising the dead, receiving divine healing from various kinds of sicknesses, experiencing financial breakthroughs, and receiving help from strangers. In other words, each one of them attested that prayer was efficient, and shared multiple examples to substantiate their claims. All of them also agreed wholeheartedly that their prayers worked because of their belief in the all-powerful name of Jesus Christ.

I was taken aback by the possibility of raising the dead through prayers, but it happened at the Living Christ Mission through the prayers of *His Grace Most Reverend (Professor) Hezekiah.* He is a man of God who shuns every effort by the people to give him credit.

"*All power, glory, and honor belong to God,*" he said during one of his sermons. He affirmed that we could do all things by faith in God through Jesus Christ. Upon further research, I found that his prayers have resulted in so many miracles that his tribesmen, the Igbos, honored him with the title *Lion of the Igbo tribe.* His country, Nigeria, also gave him the national honor of *Member of the Order of the Federal Republic (MFR).* Indeed, there were lots of evidence that overwhelmed me to quickly conclude, without any fear of contradiction, that prayer works and that anyone who calls on the name of God through Jesus Christ will receive salvation irrespective of where the person is in life.

CHAPTER 22

Area of Authority for Humanity

The Holy Spirit convicts, but does not judge;
He guides us into all truths.

Do you remember how uncle Bryan poured alcoholic drinks on the ground? He called it libation, a way of reaching out to *Ala*, which refers to the land on which we walk, in the Igbo language. Because of Igbo linguistic variations, other Igbos refer to *Ala* as also *Ali*, *Ani*, *Ana*, and by other names. *Ala* is a highly revered deity in Igbo cosmology. Uncle Bryan and my ancestors, including all Igbos who understand the Igbo cosmology, believe that the Earth is the domain given to humanity by our creator. That explains why they pour libation to invoke spirits and activate the powers inherent in the ground, to enable them to reach *Chineke*, God the creator. In many parts of Africa, people perform specific rituals to appease the land before tapping resources from the earth. I have seen

European and American miners and various types of engineers delay exploratory activities and the excavation of soils in many countries in Africa to wait for natives of the areas to perform essential rituals. These experts believe that such observances are intended to appease the powers controlling the fields before they launch their operations. After His process of creation, God placed men and women on the Earth. He gave them dominion over other inhabitants of the planet.

While I agree that other inhabitants of the Earth, such as animals, trees, and other natural resources, deserve to exist without interference from human beings, they are under the control of men and women. God is a Sovereign who does not want to rule alone because He is love, and we know that love is not selfish. So, He made men and women the caretakers of the Earth as well as everything in it. As a result, God expects humanity to occupy Earth, a position similar to His place in Heaven. Indeed, God positioned humanity to exercise His authority in the physical world we call Earth while He rules in heaven, an unseen world. In other words, Earth is an area of administration for humanity. Because living in Heaven and on Earth involve the exercise of authority and power, we can liken the Earth to what happens when a country establishes a diplomatic mission overseas. The Earth is like a place that represents the authority of heaven, and God expects us to fulfill His dominion mandate on Earth. There is a mediator known as the Holy Spirit. He facilitates communication between humanity and God. Men and women can also talk to God through prayer. The Holy Spirit reprimands us when we err, but instead of judging us, He guides us into the truth. The above arrangement sounds like the banter we hear from Christians, but it is much more significant than Christianity, and it is not about religion. It is an arrangement of the Kingdom of God, which empowers anyone who calls on His name to receive salvation.

Ironically, the work of the Holy Spirit reminds me that those who pour drinks on the ground are also communicating through the medium of spirits. As strange as it sounds, it should not be surprising, because we live in the age of spirits. As such, men and women need to identify the spirit with whom they are accomplishing their communicative role. While uncle Bryan understood the role of *Ala* in his effort to reach his creator and ancestors, can everyone say with confidence that they know the spirit with whom they are working? Uncle Bryan knew the spirit he was working with so well that he considered *Ala* to be the deity in charge of morality. To him and his cohorts, *Ala* also took charge of creativity and fertility. He believed *Ala* judged human actions, and thereby behaved like one in charge of the Judicial arm of the Igbo traditional society. As the deity in charge of fertility, *Ala* is believed to have possessed a womb where the dead slept. Similarly, *Ala* uses her fruitful belly to make the land productive, so farmers could have a bountiful harvest. Indeed, uncle Bryan is knowledgeable in the capacity and capabilities of the spirit to which he dedicated his whole life.

Humanity needs to understand that we now live in the age of the spirit. As such, anyone who wants to steer his or her mind toward better outcomes should realize the pivotal role of the Holy Spirit. Before now, the Holy Spirit came on people to make them prophesy or do other things that are usually beyond human capability, after which He leaves. In this day and age, He lives in us. He alone can purify our thoughts to make us think as Jesus intended for us. For example, the Bible did not record Jesus hearing from His father. He once said that he does what he sees His Father do. Mind you that Jesus and His Father are One. As such, the implication is that Jesus has trained His mind and thought pattern to mirror or reflect the thought patterns of His father, which means that He feels like His father. Indeed, His essence is in perfect alignment with that of His father. So, for us to live the life of our expectations and tap into the strength to do all things through Him who strengthens us, we have to start thinking as He does. It is also okay to be led by what you know, such as your five senses, which made uncle Bryan pour alcohol on the ground.

The problem, however, is that most of the things you know are not what will steer your mind to better outcomes. Everything Jesus did was a means to an end. His end or objective was to make us clean, whole, and worthy again so the Holy Spirit could abide in us once again to restore our relationship with our Source. Remember that we lost the Holy Spirit at the same time we lost our connection with our Source, which was prompted by the fall of Adam. The work of Jesus was to prepare the way for the return of the Holy Spirit. He did this successfully. All that is left now is for us to integrate ourselves into His redemptive plan, which can redeem our thoughts. If your thinking is redeemed and appropriately aligned, you will see things differently and steer your life to your desired destination.

Another thing to remember is that Jesus worked because the Holy Spirit ministered to Him directly. To show that Jesus paid all the necessary prices, imagine when He did the same thing, as God did in Genesis. God breathed into Adam (and by extension all of us) after forming him from the dust. His fall ended that era. Upon resurrection and accomplishing all the necessary work for our redemption, Jesus breathed into some folks. Afterward, they received the Holy Spirit, and He told them to go to certain places and wait for power. As you read this book, you can comport yourself and quietly invite Him into your life if you have not done so already. The invitation does not involve any complicated process. Speak and ask Him to come. There is excellent power in the spoken word, so go ahead and speak. Ask Him to dwell in you and order your thoughts. Upon entering your life, He will give you the power to steer your mind toward better outcomes, because through Him you can do all things.

Before doing that, He will help you to realize that your life has a vision, which is a product of His purpose for creating you. I know that every time the Holy Spirit manifests Himself among humanity, there is a task He wants to accomplish. He has plans, and His plans stand firm through generations. The moment you realize that God created you with the intention of doing great things, you question yourself in the manner that has been advocated throughout this book — asking the right questions. Questions such as, *"Am I merely a product of sexual intercourse by some people I did not have a prior agreement with to get me here?" "Why do I gravitate towards some things some members of my society find repulsive?"* and *"Is there more to life than eat, sleep, wake, and work?"* As you ask these and similar questions, He will help you see that you were born at the appropriate time with a purpose specifically designed to subsist for the duration of your lifetime. The fun part of purpose comes with the discovery that God has also completed all the prerequisites for you, and all that remains is for you to follow your path. That is why He said He put life and death before you, and advised you to choose life so you could live.

Another aspect of the situation is that you do not lack any required material for steering your mind towards a better outcome, and you already have the vision for fulfilling the purpose of your life. That is what He does. He leads you to all truths, remember? Are there right thoughts that will not go away from your mind? Are there tasks you will complete willingly without worrying about a paycheck? If you answered in the affirmative, you already have your vision. The next course of action should be to have Him direct your steps. Do you know that a walking man is not the one who directs his steps? Yes, he is not, because there is a way that seems right to a person, but the end of such a road is destruction. Does that bring joy to your heart? If it does, you have experienced the visitation of the Holy Spirit. If it does not, you may want to consider reading this chapter all over again because the Holy Spirit will never fail. For those who have His joy call on things that are not as if they are. Acquaint yourself with the idea that you are capable of doing all things through Him who strengthens you. Remember that He can do infinitely more than you can ask or imagine, according to His power in you. Note the previous sentence; it says that His strength is in you. As a mediator between God and us, He leads us into all truths, and you already have the ability.

Most importantly, you are on Earth, an area under the authority of humans. So, take action and exercise control without any hesitation, but not like uncle Bryan. We should learn to live our lives within the parameters God established in the Bible. Such a lifestyle will make us vessels that are useful to Him at any time. Remember that

God has an excellent track record in working with human beings to achieve His goals on Earth. The likes of Biblical Esther, who He used to preserve His people, and Moses, who rescued His people, are some of many we can emulate.

CHAPTER 23

Think Like He Does

One man forgave the sins of many.

Envision a school as a money dispenser or a soda machine, and keep in mind how, sometimes, those dispensers act funny. There are times we shake the soda machine to dispense soda. Also, we sometimes gaze at money machines after they swallow our cards or issue us with receipts that say how much money we have collected, whereas we did not receive any cash. It is worse when one is using an unfamiliar card in an overseas money machine. Like such machines, most of the knowledge they dispense at schools is downright confusing. I have noticed that such knowledge varies from field to field. For example, they tell you in some areas about how things will be in the long run, but after a long wait, you realize that the long run will never come. In the same field, they also tell you about how things will be when everything becomes equal. However, all things are hardly equal in life. In one area of knowledge, they tell us that watching movies has a disastrous long term effect on children. They go as far as saying that some of those effects can linger from adolescence and into adulthood.

One example they give is from watching horror movies. They teach us that watching such videos can be harmful even when those who are watching are aware in their hearts that the film is not real. They suggest that the human body and physiological sensors react to horror scenes as if they are real.

"Are you sure?" I once asked my professor in a graduate class.

"Yes, the mind knows what is real and what is not real, unlike your body and physiology. That is why you scream and close your eyes in a movie theater while gasping for breath with rapid heartbeats, sometimes the effect lingers for years," he replied. After he noticed the strange look on my face, he added a caveat.

Such an outcome may not apply in all circumstances. I called it shaking the knowledge machine. I grew up in Nigeria at a time when the Nigerian military held sway of the political leadership of the country. They promulgated mostly draconian decrees, and Kangaroo court systems were in place. As such, I witnessed the army shoot convicted criminals on multiple occasions as a child. It was like a fanfare.

Shootings were often announced on radio, with the time

and location of the firing squad clearly stated. We usually went in groups from our school hostel to the makeshift shooting range at stadiums or other public places to watch the execution. Members of the Nigerian military were merciless and ruthless; they also subjected coup plotters to the firing squad. They court-martialed their childhood friends who participated in failed coups and sentenced them to death by firing squad. Although I was at the age of puberty then, I knew that the shootings were real. I also knew that I was not watching a horror movie. Nevertheless, I did not find the experience entertaining. Even now, I also do not consider any shooting experience entertaining. I did not know the differences that existed between my body, mind, and physiology then. Now, I know how my body, mind, and physiology differ in orientation and reaction, yet I continue to find experiences that involve shooting repulsive. I react to similar scenes now the same way I responded to them as a teenager. There is no need to shake a knowledge machine. As a teacher, I search for sound knowledge. I seek for an education that can stand the test of time to share with my students. I found one in the Bible, a book I once viewed as a tool of capitalism.

Now, I know what the problem was. It was my approach. I approached the book with an already made-up mind, the type you have when your heart is in a negative mode. The position of my mind was not my only problem. I was also alone, but not in the sense of being by myself. I was alone because I relied on my intellectual strength as a scholar. Now, I know that by strength shall no man prevail. I have also come to understand that nothing succeeds in life because someone does something or has the ability to do so. Humanity thrives because God shows mercy. Most importantly, He sent the Holy Spirit to teach me His word as He has done to many people. However, my gratitude goes to my student, whose gentle and unassuming approach to evangelism spurred me to question myself and revisit my conclusions about life. As I write this, he is yet to know the impact his short visit to my office years ago had on my psyche and life, in general. Now, I know that the Bible is a machine that dispenses knowledge, which does not require a helpful jostle.

Biblical content enables us to believe that Jesus is the Christ, the Son of God. Also, it helps us to understand that by believing in Him, we will have life. An essential step in believing is to establish a relationship with God, who first reached out to us through His Son, Jesus. To do that, we have to accept Jesus as the Messiah, as the Son of God, and as our Savior. It is essential to understand that Jesus came with the grace to deliver us from the powers of sin and death. Men and women of today cannot save themselves. As such, they need Jesus, because He manifests the righteousness of God. Most people erroneously see Jesus as one of the prophets or another son of God, whereas He is the only Son of God, sent to reveal His Father to humanity. Jesus forgave us all our sins. He is God, not a prophet.

In the past, I did not understand much about sinning, but now, I fully comprehend that the moment we repent and ask Jesus Christ in faith to forgive us our sins, we will receive His forgiveness through grace. Do you remember the cross? He carried our sins to and on the cross. He was one man who bore the sins of all men. He cleaned our slates and gave us a fresh start in life. Until we have that fresh start, we cannot steer our minds to better outcomes.

After the fresh start, we should also start to live without sin because sin creates a barrier between us and God. Yes, it is possible to live without sin. Why do you not drive on the wrong side of the road? The answer is simple: you are not insane. This scenario applies to the kingdom lifestyle. We are able to discern what is right and what is wrong. So, let us not wait for someone to tell us to choose the right thing. You are a child of God who has been reconnected with your Father. You are from God, and you are born of the Lord. The implication is that sinlessness is in your essence, and you are holy. As such, it is within your capacity to live a godly life; no one born of God continues to sin as the seed of God is in that person. He or she cannot continue to sin. Granted, we live in a sinful world, yet it is clear that we are not of the world. Another essential aspect of following Him is that we should learn to forgive others.

Because God has forgiven us, it is only fair that we also forgive those who have wronged us. As we forgive others, we should also forgive ourselves and avoid the temptation of self-condemnation. Finally, we should ask Him for the power to face the future. He counts us righteous because of the imputation of His atoning death. Also, He makes us righteous through the impartation of His life of victory. Speaking of the successes that comes from Him, we should rest assured in the knowledge that we are not only saved but that we are saved to the uttermost.

We are not conquerors; we are more than conquerors. We will not triumph sometimes; we will triumph everytime. He will not offer us help sometimes; He will give us what we need in an exceedingly abundant manner, above all we imagine. Also, at all times, we will be filled with the fullness of God to enable us to see things as He does. As a child of God who has been reconnected to his or her Father and now perceives things as He does, you will know two things. The first is that you are from God, and the second is that you are born of the Lord. The implication is that sinlessness is your essence, and you are inherently holy. Indeed, you will not continue to sin because even though we live in a sinful world, we are not of the world. Our goal should be to think as He does. Our hearts should realize that He longs for us. We should believe in Him and accept His words as they are documented in the Bible in obedience. Then we should claim all that He has promised us because obeying Him is the way to steer our minds to our desired outcomes. By so doing, He will catapult us into positions of eminence. He once told those who were fishing to follow Him, and they obeyed. This simple act of obedience changed their lives, and they became fishers of human beings. It is possible to enjoy such benefits in the 21st century, but we have to obey Him first and follow Him.

We ought to also understand that we cannot obey or experience Him without believing in the pivotal role of His name. His name is the key. To find more about His name, we have to engage His word as documented in the Bible. We should not approach His word with human wisdom and understanding. We should instead seek the wisdom that comes from Him.

Do you remember Solomon? He enjoyed God's wisdom, which helped him govern his people effectively. God's wisdom helps us to make the right choices. Also, we should allow the Holy Spirit to guide us into His word and to reveal what lies beyond the letters of His scripture. By doing so, He will grant us His peace and joy, which surpasses all human understanding. He will put your life in order and make you taste the satisfaction that comes from Him alone, which is unobtainable elsewhere without surrendering to Him. Indeed, let us go to Him for strength because we can only successfully steer our minds to our desired outcomes through belief in Him.

CHAPTER 24

Love As He Does

Out of love, He gave His life for us.

*F*or some reason that I am not able to articulate or put in black and white, I continue to have the same impression that I have gotten since the day my student visited me in my office. This time it centers on love and seems to be saying, *"Out of the love He has for us, He died for our sins. Although He does not have any wrongdoing, He took the sins of all."*

"So, how is that my business?" I queried.

"His actions are examples for you to follow," the voice-like impression whispers.

"He suffered so you could have a credible model to follow," He continued.

Okay. Such a lifestyle offers a remarkable legacy, I thought to myself.

Someone who did not have any sin in word, deed, or thought, yet remained calm in the face of many temptations, is worthy of emulation. I know how easy it is for someone to claim to be righteous and without sin. It is as easy as just speaking, but will people take such a person seriously? How about those who are well acquainted with anyone claiming to be righteous?

For such people, it will be a hard sell because those who are close to us are often aware of our weaknesses. Unlike Jesus, those closest to Him, such as those who traveled and ate with Him, testified to His righteousness. Such people were also willing to die because of their belief in Him, especially His sonship and position as the Savior of the world. Ironically, those who were not with Him also agreed that He was a sinless man. Such people included the thief on the cross, the Centurion, and Pilate, who declared that he found no fault in Him and that He was a righteous Man, respectively.

However, *it is tough to compare the time He lived in to the 21st century. We are living in a different dispensation. Technological advancements have been propelled, so much so that most of what humanity once referred to as problems no longer qualify as such. More people are free now, and humanity has broadened their horizons to such an extent that some people no longer see barriers in life. We are in an age where some humans have dedicated their entire lives to learning. Such individuals seek solutions to issues that confront humanity. Walls and barriers are crumbling while countries are forging economic and political ties. Indeed, sovereignty now has a new meaning because there are thin lines separating countries from one another. Most im-*

portantly, values have changed tremendously. Given the differ-
ences and massive changes between now and the period during
which He lived on Earth, how can one live a lifestyle that mirrors
the examples of Jesus?

The impression seems to have a simple answer to the above question: *"Love humanity just as Jesus did."*

It sounded simple, yet I did not understand the notion. As an educator, I earn a living by imparting knowledge, but so much happens behind the scenes before I engage in the process of knowledge impartation. For instance, I read and reread notes. I plan, conduct research, evaluate, revise, and draw from appropriate strategies to drive instruction before I teach. So, I have done all that, and now, I see loving humanity the way He did as easy. Loving our fellow men and women as Jesus does is as easy as it has always been. His word teaches us empathy, forgiveness, and love. His standard requires us to respect one another while maintaining a personal relationship with Him. As such, we must understand that it is not our place to judge those who are unlike us. In spite of our differences, we reflect His image. He alone has the right to judge others. Our responsibility is to work alongside our fellow men and women with respect. We should also share our faith and pray for those who are struggling. Another way to put this is that Jesus taught us to be loving. As such, we should love our neighbors, be understanding, forgiving, and tolerant. We should also remember that everyone is our neighbor. We should, by all means, avoid being judgmental.

There is also a more straightforward and more uncomplicated way to put it: Being like Christ is achievable. You should first understand that He lived and taught love, forgiveness, how to be non-judgmental, and how to pray. There is no need to advertise your Christlike nature or boast about your righteousness. It's our connection with Him that is important. We should not attach labels to the truth or give them narrow interpretations or religious coloration. It is important to note that religions are man-made. Jesus was not a Christian, and there was not even a Bible during His time. Our Lord and Savior Jesus had a direct relationship with God, and that is what He expects from us because we are also sons and daughters of God.

Being like Him reminds me of having dual citizenship and being a legal resident of a third country at the same time. I am related to those three countries. I owe them allegiance. In turn, I have expectations from them. Yes, there are so many things I can legitimately ask from all of the countries. In one state, I have folks that I am connected with by blood. In the second state, there are people I share ideological bonds with, like the idea that humans are created equal.

As such, I can demand good governance from these two countries because even while I am overseas, I am directly affected by what is occurring in both countries.

However, without the third country, I would not be able to talk about the first two countries, because it is the third country that offers me a platform to engage in the economic activity that makes me beat my chest and call myself a man. I say so because it would have been difficult for me to fulfill such an obligation of citizenship as payment of taxes in the first two countries if the third country had not offered me gainful employment and enabling business climate for consultancy. Such an advantage explains why I cheerfully pay taxes in the three countries. Also, I consider myself a representative of these three countries wherever I go. At all times, I have documentation that shows my affiliation with these countries. So, I do my best to act appropriately when I am in one country to avoid bringing disrepute to the other two countries.

To be like Him, one must see himself or herself as being in the world but not of the world. Unlike me, who calls three countries home, we live on Earth, but our home is not here. We are merely present to influence the world. To do this, we need to be like Him. Why should we impact the Earth, you may ask? Because the planet belongs to our Father. Yes, the whole land belongs to our Father, and He has bestowed us to be caretakers. We should always remember that the Earth is the Lord's and all that dwells therein. As such, we own the planet by inheritance and responsibility. That is why He made us not only caretakers but also gave us dominion over the land. To be like Him, we must see ourselves as managers of the planet. He is a righteous father who allows His children to manage His items. He has made us kings and rulers of the world. He has given us dominion and power over the physical realm.

No wonder we call Him King of kings. We are the kings for whose King He is.

Unlike me, who worries about maintaining a good relationship with multiple countries, our responsibility should be to represent His kingdom in this world, whereas His duty is to take care of us. He has described us as sons of God as well as sons of the Kingdom. Such a privilege is not the exclusivity of any religious group. You can key into the sonship and kingdom life by believing in Jesus Christ, the most powerful name on Earth, irrespective of your religious affiliation. You may be a Buddhist, Christian, Muslim, Hindu, non-religious person, an adherent of primal-indigenous religion, or one who practices African or Asian traditional religion. You are a part of humanity, and God is interested in restoring humanity to Himself; that is all that matters. Our goal should be to love the world and bring the world back under God's control. Remember that He loved the world so much that He gave it His only begotten son. Our role is to work toward reconciling the world with God. We can accomplish this by being lovers, not haters. We are reconciliatory agents, which reminds me of Apostle Paul, who calls us ministers of reconciliation. We are to teach the nations about His principles and make disciples of them. Remember what He said to them, that all authority in heaven and on Earth had been given to Him, after which he implored them to go and make disciples of all nations.

After that, He instructed us to baptize in the name of the Father, and of the Son, and the Holy Spirit. Hold your breath, we are also to teach others to obey everything He has commanded. He ended it with the firm promise that He is always with us to the very end of the age. Sometimes we view the commission to make disciples as the prerogative of specific people. It is not. Our Lord's great commission explains what all believers should do. Engaging in evangelism should be the hallmark of every child of God. All of us should get in line and lead our fellow men and women back to their Father. However, some people often wonder how they can carry out an assignment of such magnitude. To begin, remind yourself that you belong to a nation. If you are unaware, a simple question will help to jog your memory: What do you do for a living?

Members of your professional group constitute a nation. Go and make disciples of them. Do you socialize with human beings? All the people you socialize with are members of a group. Show them through your behavior that He is waiting on them to come home. Are there some humans with whom you share ideological bonds? Do you go to school with human beings? Such people also constitute a nation. Inform them of God's salvation through Jesus Christ.

Indeed, you have the opportunity to make disciples for Him at any time of the day regardless of your location, because discipleship comes in many forms. It is fantastic if you find yourself among people. Under such a circumstance, simple things like sharing a tweet, post, or video on your cell phone (like my student did) become pathways to lead someone back to the knowledge of Kingdom principles. It helps to realize that two is better than one. So, make people comfortable around you. When you share the good news with people, avoid arguments, because we hardly learn in the presence of discord. Even if you are in a profession that requires you to prove or give evidence to advance your point of view, discard it for His sake. Do not prove anything, for He will make a name for Himself. Witness with love and point out the importance of others. Please, share with others the idea that we need each other. Show people that you sincerely appreciate their attention and make a genuine effort to love them as Jesus loves us.

Finally, as you strive to love as He does, remember that your attitude speaks more than your words. As such, you should align your behavior with your words. Also, do not be afraid to show off His power. Jesus told us that once we set the message of His kingdom rolling, the gates of hell shall not prevail against it. So, begin to set the ball rolling from wherever you are right now. Infiltrate every corner and be a witness of His glory and saving power — work towards influencing and impacting the world. In the course of making disciples of all nations, we should make it clear to folks that identifying with Him is a quicker way to steer one's mind towards desired outcomes. Indeed, having a personal relationship with God infuses His power into our lives. With His power, we have everything we could ever wish for in life. Imagine a God who chose not to spare His Son's life, but had Him die for our sins. Would it be difficult for Him to give us the desires of our hearts? God longs for us to take Him by His word and claim His power, because therein lies the road to victory in life. In fact, by loving as He does, we will overcome the world, like He did.

CHAPTER 25

New Beginning: From Darkness to Light

Humans should not be ashamed to peek before they decide to start living the life God intended for them.

A traditional belief, popular in many parts of Africa, is that a man or woman finds meaning, fulfillment, or significance in life only when he or she forges bonds with other human beings. Such reasoning is not about strictly adhering to communal life at the detriment of the wider society. Those who hold such a view owe allegiance to the broader community while also maintaining strong ties to their kith and kin. In the Igbo society for example, when a young adult member of a village has completed his or her college education, obtains a white-collar job in a city, and is ready to venture from home, immediate and extended family members give him or her a small child as company. This newly minted college graduate is expected to play dad and mom by caring for and enrolling the child in school.

The goal is for the one who has a white-collar job to carve a path for the child to follow.

The same applies to those who have successful businesses and individuals who are newlyweds. Without asking for your input or opinion, everyone in the community expects you to take someone from your family tree or your tribe to your place of business or new home. Anyone chosen for business purposes is known as an apprentice because he or she ends up learning the business skills or trade secrets of their masters or madams. For the recently married, the kids they bring with them work as house helps and help to cater to newborn babies as a way of building character. Similarly, the apprentices combine their duties of aiding in the prosperity of their preceptor's business and learning business education with character development. They engage in domestic activities such as house cleaning, car washing, and doing laundry for their madams or masters while learning how to respect the elderly and cohabit with others.

Amidst all of this, there is a tacit understanding that after several years, the business person will compensate his or her apprentice(s) and aid them financially in starting up businesses. Such an investment comes after the apprentice has developed a good work ethic in business and non-business areas. The boy and girl who joined the newly married couple will end up having their school fees paid, be appropriately raised, and eventually get married themselves. The rationale for such a traditional arrangement in the Igbo society is for anyone who is first to see the light at the end of the tunnel to preach to others believed to be in darkness. Thus, it is customary for anyone who has attained success in any area of life to show others what he or she did and the exact path they followed to succeed.

Because of this time-honored expectation, I went home to introduce the Kingdom knowledge to my family members, including my grand and great grandparents, and members of my tribe. An elderly member of the community told me that it was better to follow the belief system of our people than mess my brains up by believing something else.

"What do you mean by that?" I asked.

"No matter how you have cured a person with a mental health condition, he or she will continue to murmur," he replied.

"So, what has that got to do with me?" I asked him even though I understood him perfectly well.

"If I tell you a proverb and also explain what I said to you, it means you are tempting me to tell my kinsmen to accompany me to your maternal home, so we can ask for a refund of the dowry we paid to marry your mother."

In the traditional Igbo society, men do not convey ideas in a straight manner. Older Igbo men are known for speaking in proverbs, which they consider the oil for digesting words.

Perplexed, I watched him as he continued to speak.

"Many years before you were born, I met a Christian preacher in Houston, Texas, who gave me the first Bible I ever owned. He was a good man, but the Bible I received from him did not make me waver from what I believe. I have been reading the Bible before you were born. I heard that one of the preacher's sons preaches better than his father. I have also heard that they now own a church that records the largest number of churchgoers every Sunday in the United States."

"Would you like us to talk about those who followed their father's footsteps and improved on the foundations of their father?" I asked politely. "I know of a prominent preacher in the Bahamas, one of the greatest that ever lived. His father was also a minister of God, but he surpassed his father's accomplishments."

"Okay, why not surpass our accomplishments in ancestral worship instead of attempting to change us?" He probed, which sent me reeling in laughter, so hysterically that I almost fell to the ground.

Our discussion helped me to notice that many people had heard about Jesus Christ at one point or the other in their lives, and many of them agreed to change their thought patterns in line with God's Kingdom principles. However, many of them did not envision God as representing light, an entity for which humanity is in dire need, because they resided in darkness. He once said that He is the light of the world, but it seems that people are searching for a switch to flip for the light to shine. Unfortunately, that is not what is required of us to see the light.

Nevertheless, I am not surprised and do not see a need to apportion blame on anyone, because the way we flip light switches has been inconsistent. In Africa and Europe, for example, you flip a switch downwards for illumination, whereas if you were in the Americas, you would flip the same switch upwards to see the light from a lightbulb. As simple as such an analogy is, many people view the Savior of humanity from the simplistic prism of a switch because He refers to himself as the light of the world. In my bid to fully understand Him, I towed the same prayer line that has become my signature since the impromptu meeting in my office with my student.

So, as usual, I added a new line: "Oh, Blessed Holy Spirit, please, show me what He means by being the Light of the world."

Upon completing my prayer, I heard the voice-like impression clearer than ever.

"As Light, He is the Knowledge for saving humanity."

"Did you say knowledge?" I inquired. "I know that humans acquire knowledge in school as I did, and some of that knowledge has been helpful for humanity. For example, our knowledge of science and technology, which we acquire from educational institutions, has made life easier for us." I continued.

"The world is in darkness, and anyone who does not

know Him lives in darkness. However, humans can obtain an abundance of life through Him, and abundant life is obtained through obedience to His teachings," the impression replied.

In other words, anyone who obeys Jesus will have light, to guide him or her to eternal salvation, in this world of darkness.

Among my people, the majority of those I spoke to about the saving grace in the knowledge of Jesus Christ were in agreement with me. I witnessed that many of them put aside ancestral worship and idolatry. I also told them that such knowledge constituted an appropriate belief literacy and that whenever they apply such teaching in their lives, they are taking what I call Belief Literacy Steps. As such, the good news is worth sharing beyond the confines of my tribal community, because God created every human being. He gave us free will and did not impose any of His ideas on us. Such liberty mirrors His wisdom. Although He is our creator, He understands that anyone can forcefully steer a horse to a river but cannot force the same horse to drink water. Thus, it is okay for humans to learn from the experiences of others before they take action. In other words, humanity should not be ashamed to peek into a book such as this, which documents someone else's trials and triumphs in partaking in God's plans. After examinations and making up your mind, you can decide to begin to live the life God intended for you.

One of the ways to show smartness is to make something positive out of another person's negative experience. It is foolish to wait until you make similar mistakes and learn the hard way. After all, no one will live long enough to make all the mistakes there are to be made in life before determining how best to position his or her life. Such understanding prompted the *Literacy of Belief*, which aims at steering the human mind from ignorance (represented by darkness) to the truths of life that Jesus represents as Light. The vision of focused individuals who live purposefully on Earth drives the *Literacy of Belief*. Such people have professed the belief that God created everyone and deposited them on earth to advance His purposes.

Unfortunately, the first man and woman failed in that mission, and by extension, the rest of humanity. Fortunately, He did not give up on us. He sent His Son Jesus to die in our place. Having paid the ultimate price, we need to reconnect to our source by proclaiming Him as Savior and embracing His teachings, so we can live righteously on earth and attain the desires of our hearts. Indeed, humanity deserves access to such knowledge of love, peace, and eternal fulfillment.

Epilogue

*H*uman beings like to sound futuristic. Perhaps, that explains why we wish for good things to happen to others. For example, we tell each other goodnight before retiring to bed even when there is nothing around us to guarantee a good night. We often go beyond wishes and compliments to say to others that good things will come their way emphatically. Some people also extend similar blessings to themselves. Most times, the things we wish or tell people are entirely out of our control, yet we continue to say them. Indeed, we are unable to guarantee what will happen in the future, but somehow, something in us makes us believe that what we expressed will come to pass in the future, as we indicated. Such an attitude persists in human life, not only out of courtesy but also because humans believe, in the depths of their hearts, that what they wish will eventually happen. Such a view is prevalent because it is instilled in our nature. We can make things happen. We can concoct things through our thoughts, words, and actions. However, we need to believe that we have what it takes to make such things happen, because belief is an essential and indispensable aspect of life. To live our lives to the fullest, we need to understand the power of belief. There is no challenge in life more significant than having to choose between the competing demands of everyday life. As such, our lives mirror our choices, and those choices are largely determined by what we believe. If your beliefs are appropriately aligned and you are aware of them, you order your steps and safeguard your life by following those beliefs, which in turn position you for success.

Given the priority of our beliefs and the vital role they play in steering our minds to success, I have, in over two decades, explored many belief systems to determine whether or not there is anything worthy of belief. I found that the object of our faith is pivotal because what we believe is central to what will happen to us. I dove into myself and attempted to anchor belief on the human mind. The scientific and technological advancements of this day and age, which show the mental improvement of today's men and women, made such a thought tempting for me. However, human nature is frail and unpredictable and, therefore, unreliable. There are lots of graven images and many sculptural objects that one can believe, but to put one's trust in an idol is useless. Such figurines stand upright, like trees, but do not speak. As such, trusting in icons and other graven images is unappealing. It is not the way to go.

I explored various religious beliefs and secret societies

but figured out that most of them were the products of fear and the quest of different men and women to manipulate others. Multiple groups and fraternities attempt to fill the void by telling others what to believe. However, I noticed that such organizations, in the long run, turned out to be cults that roped people into mental enslavement through psychological manipulation. My quest then led me to the stark truth that humanity did not get here as a result of some loud noise or through many changes from being part of primates millions of years ago. Someone created us as men and women and put us on the Earth as representatives. He made the Earth by His powers. He established the world by His wisdom. He created us in His image. He gave us the ability to call unto things that are not as if they are, which explains why we are futuristic. As we wish or tell people about the good things that will happen to them in the future, we act like our Father, who created us. Yes, God created us, and we did not get here through evolution or some loud noise in someone else's backyard.

Because we are a reflection of His image, we can steer our minds to our desired destination by following the steps outlined in His principles, which constitute *Belief Literacy Steps*. Having such an understanding makes us proficient in the *Literacy of Belief.*

Acknowledgments

This work is the product of a lifetime of learning from many sources. Thanks to everyone for giving me more than I bargained. Special thanks to my daughters, Nnennaya and Enyinnaya, for using their brilliance to make my thoughts readable. I am proud of them. I hope they continue to remember my definition of a father's love and what gives Daddy the greatest joy.

I am very grateful to 12 of my former students who read this work through what they called crowd-reading. Your disagreement over the English we should use reminded me of being your teacher. From American to British and Nigerian English, all of you insisted on having the book represent Englishes. I am also fascinated by your decision to allow grammatical and typographic errors in the work to show our imperfection.

My friends at Regent press, including Mark, were super helpful. Considering the location of all the people who worked on this book, I know that we could not have done much without Google Internet-related services and products. As such, I thank the people behind Google for their foresight.

I implore all of you to understand that this is our book. Nevertheless, I accept responsibility for all errors, visible and invisible, in this work.

Connect With Uju

Uju is passionate about people and what they believe. As an explorer of belief, he is excited about meeting people of different backgrounds and learning about their beliefs.

He would love to hear from you if you choose to email him at info@literacyofbelief.com

You can also follow him on Twitter @ujucukwuoma.

If you are interested in having Uju come to your event, he is available to inspire your audience.

About The Author

Outside of college teaching and research, Uju is a volunteer board-chairman for the Association for Health & Sexual Awareness (AFHESA), a nonprofit that studies how gender identity and sexual orientation influence behavior and educational attainment. AFHESA explores the intersection of belief, gender, and popular culture in decision-making to facilitate responsible sexual choices for adolescents.

He is also working on a volunteer basis as the principal consultant for the *Literacy of Belief* LLC, a team of experts who are enthusiastic about helping educational authorities around the world improve literacy standards. His team is also involved in coaching people in the area of belief, provision of corporate training, and development management. Uju lives in Houston, Texas, in the United States of America.

CPSIA information can be obtained
at www.ICGtesting.com
Printed in the USA
FSHW021627050920
73507FS